WOMEN ENTREPRENEUR REVOLUTION:
Ready! Set! Launch!

100+ Successful Women Entrepreneurs Share Their Best Tips
on What Works, What Doesn't (and Why) When You're
Launching a Business and Designing a Life You Love

JENN AUBERT

BALBOA.
PRESS

A DIVISION OF HAY HOUSE

Balboa Press books may be ordered through booksellers or by contacting:

Balboa Press
A Division of Hay House
1663 Liberty Drive
Bloomington, IN 47403
www.balboapress.com
1 (877) 407-4847

Printed in the United States of America.

ISBN: 978-1-4525-9439-2 (sc)
ISBN: 978-1-4525-9441-5 (hc)
ISBN: 978-1-4525-9440-8 (e)

Library of Congress Control Number: 2014904949

Balboa Press rev. date: 03/21/2014

To my very first role model, my mom, who believed in living life with "no regrets."

CONTENTS

PART THREE: Stepping Up Now That You've Arrived
How your success will change your life and the lives of others.

Thanks!

When I first started writing this book I had no idea where this project would take me. It has been absolutely the best, most inspiring and energizing experience I've had the courage and privilege to undertake.

Thanks to each of the one hundred amazing and accomplished women who took the time to share their stories. You inspired me with your insight, stories and graciousness. Thank you for encouraging me to stay the course. I feel truly blessed to have had the chance to meet you.

Thank you to my fabulous editor, Pamela Schott, who took a chance on me very early on and who has been my right-hand woman throughout this process. Thank you for your honesty, generosity and guidance. I could't have done this without you.

Thanks to the hard-working and dedicated team at Balboa Press who made my dream become a reality.

Thanks also goes to my gal posse, my creative collective (whatever we decide to call ourselves this week), Giselle Shardlow, Karen Hancock, and Tina Delaney who cheered me on every step of the way. Thanks also to my dear friend Cortney Devlin who jumped in at the end and introduced me to a network of women I didn't even know existed.

Thanks to each and every one of my dearest and closest friends and family who took an interest, expressed excitement, provided suggestions and introductions and supported me during this journey. Love to you all.

And finally with immense love, gratitude and devotion I dedicate this book to my adorable son, Finn, and my husband, Steve Noveshen, who's love and unshakable belief in all my crazy pursuits makes everything possible.

INTRODUCTION

It's the End of the World As We Know It...

In case you haven't heard, there is a revolution occurring, and it's happening right now.

It may not be loud or confrontational.

There may not be people marching in Washington or protesting in the streets, and chances are good you won't see placards or hear chants from booming bullhorns.

This revolution is a subtler one, but no less powerful.

And it starts with a single woman.

A woman who has an idea and is feeling the pull to boldly take it out into the world.

A woman who isn't protesting anything other than the status quo and the outdated notion of working for someone else.

A woman who's standing with one foot propped against the door, holding it open to allow a flood of women to join her. And, they have.

This revolution is about freedom.

Choice.

Opportunity.

This revolution is entrepreneurialism.

...Yes, Indeed.

In June 2012, a *Forbes* article written by Natalie MacNeil entitled, "Entrepreneurship Is The New Women's Movement" was shared instantly across social media platforms and spoken about in women networking groups. Concurrently, heavy-hitting women such as Sheryl Sandberg, Chief Operating Officer at Facebook and Anne-Marie Slaughter, Professor of Politics and International Affairs at Princeton University were giving inspiring and thought-provoking talks on the state of women in the work place. Sandberg noted how women were opting out of career tracks and "leaning" back rather than "leaning in." Slaughter raised the question whether or not women "can have it all."

The answer, according to the Dr. Slaughter, is sadly "no."

In fact, both women spoke on how employers are losing valuable talent as a result of inflexible working conditions. Their comments and criticisms focused primarily on women who were on the corporate track. Little, however, has been written on women who have jumped off the corporate track (or who have never opted in to begin with) to start ventures of their own.

MacNeil's *Forbes* article started a rally cry that was heard from San Francisco to Sydney. To women from across the country and around the world, entrepreneurialism provided the answer they were seeking. Here was their chance to bring their creative ideas to fruition, while creating flexibility in their lives and driving their own career paths — without relying on a company to chart their course or a partner with a substantial income.

And today, the statistics are looking even better.

Currently, there are over eight million women-owned businesses in the U.S.

That's more than the population of New York City.

What's more, it is estimated that women will create over half of the nine-million new small business jobs by 2018. Many of these businesses will be micro (less than five employees) or small businesses.

As women meander the lonely path of business ownership, they need to equip themselves with the tools and resources necessary to succeed. The economic climate, the low barriers to entry and the pervasiveness of technology have set them up for success.

In fact, the only thing that could potentially hold these creative and ambitious ladies back are themselves.

This is a new territory for many women, and the road can be fraught with potholes and roadblocks that can flatten a woman's resolve in a New York minute. As women begin to look around for examples of other women succeeding in business, they're finding a draught of adequate female role models through the media and other typical sources of information.

Not so for women in the corporate world, who need only to look to inspiring role models such as Facebook's Sheryl Sandberg, Yahoo! CEO Marissa Mayer, or Pepsico's Indra Nooyi.

But ask most women to list the marquee names of female entrepreneurs, you often get a shoulder shrug or the standard "go-to" answer: Oprah.

Oprah? Really?

Where are all the successful women entrepreneurs hiding? If there are more than eight million women-owned businesses in the U.S., why don't we have at least a handful of ladies whose names dash out of our mouths when asked, "Who are your role models in the entrepreneurial space? Who do you admire?"

Entrepreneurial success isn't taught in school. If you're industrious enough (or an information geek like I am), you can go to the library and collect dozens of books — mostly written by men about men — to glean some answers. And while it's true that you can research and find an occasional biography or article about high-profile women who've successfully reached certain financial milestones there still remains few models to learn from. If you have few or no examples to draw on and you lack the basic tools, mindset and behaviors, choosing entrepreneurialism is like jumping into this already risky adventure with a blindfold on and your hands and feet tied. You leap with the hope that things will 'work themselves out,' but last I looked, that isn't the smartest way to start a business.

Why I Wrote this Book

I wrote this book for women who want a shot at being wildly successful.

A chance to shine in whatever field their hearts are calling them to pursue, to whatever extent.

An opportunity to make their own way, and follow their own lights.

I wrote this book for you.

I want you to whole-heartedly know you're not alone in this amazing adventure. There are women everywhere to draw on for inspiration, mentorship and guidance. They walk amongst us. You might even know them personally but have neglected to stop and notice that they had something valuable to share.

In the last 30 years, we women have built a ridiculously high pedestal for those we term "role models" and have raised them to hero-like status. How helpful is it to only admire a select few people who are so untouchable that their lives and achievements seem grandiose and in many ways unattainable?

But what if we were to drop the bar and allow more people to be role models for us to learn from?

I invite you to consider something that might make you incredibly uncomfortable. This may be a stretch for you — especially if you're just starting out in business — but I would like to propose that you start your venture with one radical intention in mind: that one day, you will be a role model for others.

Just in case you're skimming the Introduction waiting to get into the juicy bits of this book I'm going to repeat it: *Start your business knowing, believing, and acting like a role model for others!*

Here's what I mean.

What if you started your entrepreneurial journey *knowing* that you could impact hundreds, thousands, or even millions of other women on this same path. Would you do certain things differently — *right now?*

Starting this journey knowing you're going to be a model for others makes savvy business sense and, more importantly, represents one of the best ways to give back.

Now, I'm not going to pretend that some of you will be on the fence about this whole "role modeling" idea. I get that.

But keep in mind that part of this book is also about learning and cultivating how successful entrepreneurs get shit done.

And that's a good thing.

Because last I checked, there isn't a gene for entrepreneurialism or business ownership (I'm sure they would have found and patented it by now if there was one) and we aren't magically born with all the skills needed to start a business. As with most things in life, you need to learn, develop and refine what you already were given.

But that's where this book comes in.

Through my research and interviews, I've identified a number of traits and behaviors that all successful women share in common that will help you start and grow a business and fast-track your chances of success. In the chapters that follow, I will share with you exactly what those factors are so that you can either shine a light on those qualities you already have (but may have been neglecting) or don't see the value in, such as creativity, integrity, or great communication skills, or even those you need more help developing, like self-promotion, networking, or how to gracefully embrace failure.

By the way, if you can't get behind the idea of calling yourself an entrepreneur, it's time you get over that. Because if you're starting any type of venture from scratch in the hopes of making an impact and money, I've got news for you: you're an entrepreneur.

And I Feel Fine

As an entrepreneur, I have always been fascinated by why some women are successful against the likeliest of odds and why others fail before they even get their ideas out the door. I've watched bright, creative women get stuck in a cycle of fear, procrastination, overwhelm and perfectionism —even though they have all the tangible skills needed to be successful. I've observed what works and what clearly doesn't work — not only in their actions, but in their mindset as well. And in an effort to understand what was going on in myself and others, I've read every business book I could get my hands on constantly noticing that most were written by men, for men.

In these books, I searched for that one delicious, secret ingredient to propel my business forward, but very few felt like they were speaking to me.

I was looking for jet fuel, and all I found were just piles of soft manure.

Most books spoke to the tactical aspects of starting a business (so boring!), but not the softer skills. The practical stuff was easy to learn. Do this, don't do that, fill out this form, hire an accountant, sign up for this social media site, incorporate, don't forget your taxes. *Got it.* But what I still didn't understand was how, once the logistics were taken care of, did people soar in this weird, wild field of business?

When I began to look around for examples of successful entrepreneurial women, I soon realized they were difficult to find. I wasn't the only one; most women I spoke to could barely list more than two or three women they admired.

But that all changed for me in Fall of 2012, when, after asking a forum of over a thousand women-business owners who their role models were and receiving only a few responses (you guessed it, Oprah came out on top —again), I knew that I needed to do something. And, quick!

I launched the Role Models Wanted Project in March of 2013. I gave myself one year to speak to one hundred female entrepreneurs in a variety of industries and geographies, research business, psychological, sociological and biological theories and write this book. Driven by my crazy passion for this topic, I took a financial risk (yes, we entrepreneurs love a dose of risk with our passion and purpose) and put my other business on hold until I completed the project.

When I started the project, I expected to be met with a lot of "no's" and unresponsive emails, but I was shocked to have women enthusiastically agree to chat with me — lovely, accomplished, and busy women who graciously answered all my questions and put me in touch with other equally amazing women. I am still in awe of their generosity.

What you now hold in your hands is a result of that twelve-month search. Consider it as a guide to help you massage, tweak and enhance the qualities you undoubtedly already have so that you can succeed not only in business, but in all areas of your life.

As you read through the chapters, it is my hope that you will draw on the stories of others who have been in your shoes and have tales to share. From their stories, may you grow in understanding of why it's so important that women like us build a community, seek out role models, mentors, and advisors, and then, in turn, become these for others.

We need to prepare ourselves for this movement. We couldn't be living in a more exciting time, and the only people that could potentially and ruthlessly stand in the way are ourselves.

So get ready.

I know how easy it is to skim through a book, nod in agreement to the bits of insight and then shelve it around page 150.

But I want something more for you.

I want for you to walk away from each chapter, eager and inspired to put what you've learned into action.

I want you to be moved by the insights and stories of others and to see yourself in these tales of success.

I want you to aspire to be your absolute best self in business and in life — not just for you, but for the women around you, and for the world.

That's a tall order, but you wouldn't have picked up this book if you didn't want that for yourself as well.

Preparing For the Journey

So this is how we're going to roll.

Women Entrepreneur Revolution: Ready! Set! Launch! is broken into three parts.

In the first part of the book you will learn why role models are important and how they can have a radically positive impact on your life. Who knew, right?

The second part of the book will dive deep into the secrets of female entrepreneurs. This is where you're going to have a lot of fun. You will discover the mindset, motivation, and behaviors that make these women wildly successful. You will also learn why your tribe and community is crucial to your success and how to keep your energy up when all signs lead to burn-out city.

This part of the book will require some thoughtful insight and reflection and to help you along your path, each chapter includes:

* Challenges: Questions to ponder and action steps to take
* Spotlights: Stories and insights from successful women entrepreneurs
* Inspiration Library: Includes movies, music and books to help fuel your journey

In the third part of the book, you will learn the #1 savvy success characteristic all these women have in common along with a few remaining challenges that trip up many women along the entrepreneurial path. Along with what you've learned in Part II, knowing these last stones that stumble the strongest of women will provide you with the strongest foundation possible for enduring success. Then we'll wrap with parting gems of advice from the one hundred women interviewed.

Are you ready for all of this?

Let's dive in, shall we?

"The world will be saved by the
Western woman."
—Dalai Lama

PART ONE:
Importance of Role Models
to Your Success

How role models can impact
your business and life.

CHAPTER 1

What's a Role Model, Anyway?

> "Is there anyone so wise as to learn by the experience of others?"
>
> —Voltaire

Before we begin our adventure together, I want you to get clear on a few basic, although convoluted, concepts.

The first concept is "entrepreneur." You, my dear, are an entrepreneur. You may vigorously shake your head in disagreement and disbelief or say to yourself "No, that's not me," but you are, in fact, a sparkling example of one. The concept is hotly debated with people trying to create definitions to exclude most everyone who is starting a venture while keeping the title as exclusive as owning an Hermès Birkin bag. However, if you are starting a business from the ground up and taking on a financial risk to do so, you are an entrepreneur. This includes the ingenious people starting social ventures in which creating innovative solutions to solve social problems is their main goal.

The second concept is "role models." This will require a bit more explanation so hold tight. Clearly, I'm a big fan of this idea; otherwise why would I ask hundreds of women about their role models, spend my treasured weekends at my alma mater's library researching its roots and spend a year dedicated, dreaming and sometimes arguing (even with myself) about its importance?

The conventional (aka boring) definition of role models doesn't quite make a strong case for its importance:

a person whose behavior in a particular role is imitated by others. (Merriam-Webster)

Few of us want to outright copy, imitate or act like anyone else; with this simple definition, the importance of role models is sadly lost. So what does one make of this whole concept of role models and why should you care anyway?

Let's face it: the term "role model" has taken an ugly and confusing turn in the last 30 years.

What once was reserved for those who held this pristine status reflecting integrity, contribution and strength has been casually tossed around to explain rock stars, sports players, celebrities and, occasionally, reality television stars. One week a particular star is celebrated as a role model for young girls, and after a late night dalliance and a flash of her unmentionables, the headline becomes "Role Model?".

How quick one is to fall from the pedestal.

But did it make sense to put her up there to begin with? What "role" are we hoping for her to model?

This casual use of the term flies counter to the individuals most people name as their personal role models. Typically, it's a "Who's Who" list of extraordinary people, including political leaders, social activists, spiritual gurus, socially conscious entrepreneurs and highly innovative business moguls: Martin Luther King, Jr., Mahatma Gandhi, Margaret Thatcher, Steve Jobs, Richard Branson, Hilary Clinton, Oprah Winfrey and Michelle Obama. That's an impressive list of public figures each possessing a coterie of talents, gifts and contributions to the world at large.

In comparing the vastly different ends of the spectrum (one of which I suspect is fueled by publicity agents and the media), it's clear we're missing a middle ground. On the one hand, we flippantly call celebrities and sports stars role models while also calling significant social and political leaders, such as the esteemed Nelson Mandela, a role model as well.

But what role are each of these people playing and what aspects are people hoping to model?

The only common thread that runs through this widely diverse list of people is the fact that they are public figures and highly visible.

With the confusion in defining and identifying role models also comes resistance to the notion altogether. Making the seemingly ridiculous suggesting that there is even a need for role models is complicated by the fact that we live in an age where authenticity and unique self-expression are the traits *du jour*.

A Very Brief History Lesson

The concept of role models has traveled a long way from its origins.

"Role model" is a recently coined term that came out of a Columbia University study of socialization of medical students in the 1950s. Robert K. Merton, fondly called "Mr. Sociology" by his students and peers, was one of the most influential sociologists of the twentieth century. He found that individuals use groups as a frame of reference to evaluate their own ambitions, achievements, aspirations and performance. He was primarily studying medical students and how they viewed other doctors to understand how to practice their craft and get ahead. Essentially, he believed that every person compares herself with every other person within a particular social or professional role that just happens to be the role they aspire to attain.

Although the term was coined in the halls of sociology, psychologists have taken a more comprehensive look at how modeling impacts individuals. The traditional concept of role model, which most definitions still reflect, is that of a person who is in an influential position, such as parents, teachers, and mentors, who provide an example for individuals to imitate. Modern researchers however, have revised the view that role models contribute to an active process where one constructs their ideal or best possible self based on their developmental needs and goals. In other words, you're trying on traits, behaviors, and qualities of people you admire to compose the ideal person you want to be. This lends nicely to a generation of those seeking self-improvement and provides an additional tool to do so.

Where Did We Go Wrong?

In speaking to hundreds of women about role models and researching how role models are portrayed in the media, there has been a strange phenomenon that has occurred over the last thirty years: we have elevated role models to a hero-like status and have often overlooked or eliminated models who may be in our own backyard. This seems to be both for personal role models as well as professional models. We require that these select individuals encompass such a vast array of character traits and embody a certain level of perfection that the number of potential women role models can be counted on one hand. They have to be professionally successful, generous, nurturing, full of integrity, courageous, outspoken, relatable, family-oriented, humble, stylish and have an inspiring back story.

When asked to name their female entrepreneurial role models, the short list that most women business owners provide are leaders who have built multi-million, and, in some cases, billion-dollar businesses. The list typically includes Sara Blakely of Spanx, Oprah Winfrey and Arianna Huffington. For some women, Martha Stewart makes this list but for many others she often misses the mark on a few of the qualities noted above.

And this makes sense.

After all, these highly visible women are on television, gracing the covers of magazines, running media companies (often named after themselves) and profiled regularly in the news. They are at the top of their game. For many newly self-anointed business women, who do not personally know business owners and entrepreneurs, looking to these women is a reasonable approach.

You have to start somewhere.

Sadly, though, these women are often the only female role models ever mentioned by women who run their own business; they are the *only* perceived role models out there for business women.

With a plethora of women launching businesses, we cannot only have a few women to draw from as examples. They cannot represent everything to everyone, nor should they.

There are many reasons why women have a tough time locating role models and, therefore, resort to relying on the high-profile, celebrity names for guidance.

For many women business owners, they may not know other women who have started a business. What's more, because many women have spent most of their own careers in traditional professional fields, examples from their own lives of women they can observe and learn from are scarce. Many do not have family members as examples, either (although research shows that you're more likely to have a parent who is an entrepreneur).

Let's face it: women are relatively new to this show, so we're only now beginning to know more and more women who have successfully launched a business of their own.

Thankfully, this will not be the case for the next generation of women entrepreneurs, if we play our cards right.

When entrepreneurs are not able to find models of success in their personal lives, they turn to newspapers, trade journals, online resources and industry magazines. In response, traditional media outlets are increasingly highlighting female entrepreneurs, but not at equal rates in comparison to their male counterparts. Every business magazines has a Top Women in Business round-up each year hoping to even the playing field. Generally women are not given equal cover exposure and features attention as men are — something that may be attributable to the perception that women start fewer businesses in sexy, high-growth industries like hedge funds or high-tech, or lead companies that produce strong revenues that attract the interest of investors, journalists and magazines.

"Can't We Just Blame The Media?"

Sorry to say, but we cannot entirely blame the media on women's lack of exposure to adequate role models.

We women are also to blame.

One issue is the fact that when it comes to revenue, business women are grossly lagging behind men. When women aren't putting up the numbers, we don't hear about them. The amount of money your company brings in is still a very prominent definition of success.

In 2010, U.S. Census statistics showed that while women-owned businesses represented nearly half of all privately-held companies, the vast majority (about 75 percent) reached less than $50,000 in annual revenues.

That's barely enough to pay themselves a full-time salary. And if you live in New York City, San Francisco or another major metropolitan city, that will just about cover your rent and coffee expense.

When looking at companies that made more than one million dollars annually, female-owned companies only represented 2.6 percent compared to 6.0 percent of male-owned firms. Many people I interviewed noted that certain women are "lifestyle entrepreneurs" — someone who builds a business with the purpose of maintaining a certain way of life rather than strictly focusing on profits — which may explain the pithy financial returns. The Internet has allowed for a whole crop of people who fall into this category to launch profitable businesses, some of whom are, in fact, making over a million a year.

Nell Merlino may disagree that lifestyle entrepreneurs are the sole cause for these low revenue figures. Nell founded Count Me In, a not-for-profit resource for women looking to grow their micro business into a million dollar enterprise and is the original creative force behind Take Our Daughters to Work Day. In numerous interviews, she notes that the disparity in revenues is due to several factors, including low self-confidence, lack of available funding and poor hiring practices.

Nell's solutions? Women need to think bigger — much bigger.

One example she often uses to illustrate her point involves a tasty sweet treat. Nell recommends that if you own a cupcake business, instead of looking to open another store, you should be looking to see how you can be the main provider of cupcakes to Starbucks.

That's big thinking. And Nell is on a mission to help women do just that through her Make Mine a Million $ Business program that helps small business women grow their revenues to a million or more annually.

Although they have great business ideas, many women think in smaller terms which, sadly, leads to smaller revenue numbers.

As we've seen, with small returns comes faint visibility — both in the media and in one's community. It's hard to locate role models when many make barely enough to cover their basic expenses.

The other reason that women role models are hard to find is that women tend to shrink from the spotlight and avoid tooting their own horns, favoring instead to put their heads down and work hard with the hope that they'll get a gold star for their work. Even the most confident women have a hard time speaking up about their accomplishments. Often we believe that if we do a good job, work hard, and produce a great product or service, we will be noticed and celebrated for our efforts.

But that assumption doesn't fly in the corporate world, and it definitely doesn't allow women to build sustainable businesses.

Why are women such notoriously poor self-promoters? From an early age, we hear from parents, teachers and society, "Don't be a show-off". We are taught that humility is a desirable quality for a lady, and that we ought to maintain this decorum both personally and professionally.

We've learned that showing off, bragging about our accomplishments or sharing our wins makes others feel uncomfortable. As the natural social creatures that women are, we are programmed to preserve the connections between ourselves and others. The female brain is literally wired for fitting in, which often gets in the way when we're running a business, pitching our products and services, or promoting ourselves.

In her pioneering book, *The Female Brain*, Dr. Louann Brizendine examines the role our brains play on our relationships, development and social-emotional behavior.

"From their earliest days, [girls] live most comfortably and happily in the realm of peaceful interpersonal connections. They prefer to avoid conflict because discord puts them at odds with their urge to stay connected, to gain approval and nurture."

Imagine how many women would shine in the world and be role models for others, if only we could learn to share our accomplishments without feeling that our actions would alienate others.

This is a two way street, though.

We have to share in our sister's wins without eye-rolling, gossiping, or thinking she's getting too big for her britches. We need to celebrate others and the risks they're taking on in the world so that we can in turn celebrate ourselves.

Why More Are Needed... and Badly!

Role models play a valuable role in understanding where we are and where we want to be in the future. They enable us to know that what we're seeking is possible and attainable. When we're talking about doing something risky, such as launching a business, it's nice to know that others have already done it successfully. People are more likely to believe that certain things are possible if they see people who are similar to them accomplishing it.

Before we start something new:

We need to know that it can be done.

We need to know that we can do it, too.

Models of success not only give us the belief of what's possible, but through learning and observing what they did to accomplish this success, can further buoy our self-confidence. They can also fast-track our own success as we learn to recognize and maneuver the challenges and obstacles that may lay ahead of us.

When you begin the journey of business ownership, you realize quickly that with this change in your daily life, finances, and time, your identity is quickly shifting and changing as well. Previously, you may have been a top dog in your company and regularly recognized for your accomplishments. You were associated with a particular title and function, such as 'Vice President of Marketing,' 'Senior Scientist,' 'Nurse,' 'Senior Sales Director' or 'Managing Partner.' Leaving those titles behind — along with the accolades, perks, benefits and a regular paycheck that come with them — can feel like a huge hit to your ego. You are out on your own — usually doing it alone. You are now wearing lots of hats, and not all of them very glamourous. You feel like you've tossed everything you are familiar with out the window and are starting your life over from scratch. It's a heavy feeling, and one that's tinged with feelings of uncertainty, fear and self-doubt.

Studies have shown that role models play a valuable role in helping form one's self-concept, which is especially important during a major transition such as this. If you're afraid that looking to more accomplished women will make you feel worse about yourself, don't worry; it has been shown that if you're goal includes "self-improvement," the positive impact of role models overwhelmingly outweighs their potential for negative comparisons.

What a relief.

As you launch out on your own, you may begin to look for mentors and models of success. It's easy to skip quickly right to the top, looking solely at the highest rungs of leadership and fame to find adequate role models for business. As we've seen, it's common to admire the business moguls who run billion-dollar companies and who we identify solely by their first name (Oprah, Ariana, Martha).

But can we identify with and relate to these accomplished women, and do we even want to?

Research has recently found that these "elite women" don't always make the most useful models, especially if you're just starting out. Crystal L. Hoyt and Stefanie Simon published an article in *Psychology of Women Quarterly* titled "Female leaders: Injurious or inspiring role models for women?". They were specifically looking at the impact that mentors have on women in leadership positions but uncovered some interesting results. They found that the elite women in organizations — those who have reached high levels of achievement — were not the most appropriate role models for early career women. Women reported greater feelings of inferiority and lower leadership aspirations. The achievement and success of the elite women seemed entirely too unattainable. Their study showed that early career women were more inspired by middle management women whose success seem more in reach. They could more easily identify with and relate to women just a few steps ahead of them on the career path. So does this mean that Oprah is out?

Don't Ditch Oprah Just Yet

Although elite role models may make us feel less confident in our abilities, it is interesting to note that they may inspire us at an unconscious level in stressful situations. A study published in the *Journal of Experimental Social Psychology* provides an interesting example of just how important role models are to women's actual performance. In the study, Ioana Latu and her colleagues asked participants to give a persuasive public speech while being subtly exposed to a photo of either Hilary Clinton, Angela Merkel, Bill Clinton or no image at all. They found that women were not only more persuasive, they spoke longer and exhibited more empowered behavior when a picture of Hilary Clinton or Angela Merkel were displayed. So keep those vision boards with photos of inspiring women close by. You may find that there mere presence is subconsciously boosting your confidence.

Although these two studies sound contradictory, one explanation for the differing results is that in the case of the women exposed to the photos on the back wall (the Clintons and Merkel), they were asked to perform a task — take action — under a stressful situation *before* they had time to evaluate their performance, whereas in the Hoyt study, the participants were presented with the elite examples prior to a particular task. This gave the ladies ample time to compare and self-assess. Women are tough self-critics, as we all know well, and it came to light in this study.

You don't need to toss the icons and celebrity gals out the window when selecting role models. They are a wonderful resources to draw on depending on what you're aspiring to become. But keep in mind that there are many other women out there that can provide fantastic models of success.

Models Of Our Very Own

Thanks to the plethora of women climbing the ranks over the last forty years and the media attention placed on these high-profile women in the last few years, our corporate sisters have luckily had role models at their disposal. Female role models from the corporate world have been on the rise, and, thanks to the likes of Sheryl Sandberg (Facebook), Marissa Mayer (Yahoo!), Ursula Burns (Xerox) and Indra Nooyi (PepsiCo), to name just a few, there are examples of women who have meandered, some propelled, to prominent positions of influence.

Thankfully, the number of female CEOs and women in the C-suite continue to rise. But we still have a long way to go to be adequately represented. There is a unique set of skills that you must possess to negotiate your way in the corporate world, and you can learn from the wide variety of role models and mentors available. Bear in mind, however, that starting your own venture requires a completely different skill set.

We, too, can draw on models from the corporate side, but we also need to identify women from the entrepreneurial set because our challenges can be quite different. There is a mindset as well as situational factors that come into play when women leap out on their own.

Whatever your situation might be, the notion of risk makes a dramatic entrance when you decide to start a business. You may have had a corporate gig or a job in a vocational field where you lived comfortably, knowing that a paycheck would appear in the bank account every two weeks and that healthcare was a given. The perceived security of a nine-to-five traditional job has been traded for the freedom of running your own show. With this massive shift from perceived security into a place of uncertainty can stir up many emotions — even in the most self-confident woman.

The vast majority of women starting their own businesses are in solo or micro (less than five employee) ventures. Some may have the support of their spouse, although few families are able to live on one income these days. A woman's income isn't for luxury trips and designer hand bags; it is often to pay for half the mortgage, their children's education, groceries and a modest family vacation. So in the case of a wife or mom starting out on her own, she may in fact be taking the whole family into risky waters. Similarly, single women, without the safety net of a partner or a trust fund, may be using their savings, cashed-out 401Ks, credit cards, or loans from family and friends. Either situation is a risky proposition with no guarantees.

Another challenge that some entrepreneurs face — those that are dubbed "mompreneurs" —involves managing the kids and a business often at the exact same time. When you don't have the income immediately flowing in to cover a nanny or extended childcare, these overtaxed women end up squeezing in chunks of time while the kids are napping or at school. They find themselves waking up long before their family rises in the morning and working late into the evening just to keep their business moving forward. They're often working alone, disconnected from others, and keeping an insane schedule.

We need examples of women that speak to us and our unique challenges. Women who are taking risks, learning as they go, raising funds, working from home, finding advisors, working with mentors, integrating family and friends while pursuing a business and life that ignites a deep-seeded passion that cannot be ignored.

Rest assured – they are out there.

The old-world view that you can just jump into starting your own business and figure it out as you go along isn't working as many women (and men) had hoped. Lately, we've been promised that entrepreneurism is the yellow brick road to freedom, abundance and living our purpose while making a living. We know that it will require a lot of work (although with books like *The 4-Hour Work Week* by Tim Ferriss, we may have been misguided that we can build a wildly successful empire in just a few hours a week while sitting on a beach sipping Coronas), but don't be mistaken; it takes work in the beginning.

A lot of work.

But the work is driven by you, and in the end, you know all the hours, sweat and tears combined provides the amazing results and ultimately gives meaning to your life. This type of purpose-driven work is much more gratifying than working forty hours a week for someone else and their dreams, that's for sure. Our kind of work pays out wild dividends in freedom, self-confidence, and success on our own terms. And quite frankly, we love the work.

The old-world views on entrepreneurism includes stacks of figures that are not encouraging and downright depressing. We all know the failure rate for new businesses is ridiculously high. It is commonly noted that in the United States, seven out of every ten new businesses fail. Based on the Bureau of Labor Statistics data, half of new businesses are gone within six years of starting. If you're lucky to make it to ten years, only about one-third of your peers are still standing with you.

If you think that is alarming, hold on to your knickers. It gets much worse than that.

In fact, for many of us solopreneurs and micro-entrepreneurs who have businesses with fewer than twenty employees, the four-year survival rate is 37 percent, and the ten-year survival rates is a measly nine percent. That's shocking and sad. And as noted previously, the women business owners who luckily stay in business don't make much to even speak about.

This doesn't need to be you. You don't have to be yet another statistic.

Fueled with the knowledge, tactics and inspiration in this book, you will look at these figures and say, "Hell, no! That won't be me."

We are living in a new world, that is for sure. And it is fast and ever-changing. This new, exciting world brings with it a whole new level of possibilities, innovative strategies to adopt and technologies not even dreamt of yet. However, we, too have to adapt to this new world. As a result of this fast-pace, independently-driven work environment that often leaves us feeling disconnected from others, we can easily drown unless we consciously take control of our inner lives and our outer world.

Whatever your situation may be, you don't have to be alone in your office wondering how others are doing it. You don't have to keep banging your head against the proverbial wall trying to figure something out that others ahead of you have already mastered. If you are not able to find out publicly through articles, videos, and interviews how others have done it, I bet they'd be happy to share with you what they've learned along the way.

You need only to ask, and invite others to stand up and share.

In this new world of interconnectedness, the women who will rise to the top will be those who master their own inner chaos, have deep connections to why they've started their businesses, are willing to share with others how they made it while continuously nurturing connections, and who stand firmly in the spotlight to be models for others. They will seek role models and will ultimately be role models themselves. This new world is calling. Are you willing to engage and shine?

CHAPTER 2

Why Do I Need a Role Model?

"We need role models who are going to break the mold."
—Carly Simon

The Power of Role Models

Some people may argue that emulating others is disempowering and produces a society of clones. I'm the first person to vehemently promote finding your uniqueness and honoring your own brilliant, authentic self. There is nothing more beautiful and alluring than a woman truly living in her own skin and living out her purpose.

Beneath all this talk of role models is the notion that in working towards finding and developing your ideal professional and personal self you are, in fact, refining the authentic person at the core.

Far from disempowering women to be uniquely their own selves, this approach is about modeling strategies and then putting your unique spin on them.

Role models are simply a tool in your lovely drawer of accouterments that you can use to learn more about the world, about your work, and about yourself. We are social creatures, and as much as the Internet makes it easy to live in a bubble believing we're super connected because our Facebook friend count is tipping over one thousand, or that we're tweeting with people we've never actually met in person, we do not thrive in isolation.

In spite of all of this connectivity, it's easy to feel disconnected and alone in our current "socially networked" landscaped, and even more so as an entrepreneur venturing forth in an unknown land. But we need to remember that the path to feeling most alive and truly thriving runs through how we relate to others — and, more importantly — ourselves.

When you look at the layers of our lovely blue globe that we call home we notice that each of the Earth's layers has a name and specific composite of minerals. Each layer supports the layer above it and blends into the layer below it.

The same is true of our relationships. Only these layers are formed of intimate connections, immediate family, extended family, best friends, close friends, acquaintances, colleagues, business partners, advisors, mentors, role models and people we just plain think are cool. Some relationships are more intimate than others. Some show up in a number of layers (such as when your business advisor also happens to be a role model). But however these relationships are defined, there is no doubt you can learn from all the individuals and each relationship can be part of your personal growth process.

When it comes to business, the strata of colleagues, peers, partners, advisors, mentors and role models can provide a plethora of insights, advice, wisdom and guidance — all invaluable tools that can help you be the most powerful, successful entrepreneur possible.

Perhaps nowhere is this most evident than in the relationships savvy women entrepreneurs forge with mentors and role models — those meant to inspire you to achieve the level of success or influence.

It is about aspiring to achieve, not aspiring to be.

The best role models don't just inspire; they instruct. For some people, their role models are not only examples of what they aspire to achieve, but are exemplary people as well. Who you consider a role model can also shift and change through the years as a result of your current state in life and in business and your continuous exposure to new people who have a lot to offer.

For example, say you're at a point in your business where you're considering fundraising. Because you realize this is an area in which you are not quite as proficient as you'd like to be, you begin to look around and find several amazing examples of women who have done a spectacular job fundraising. You get advice, you chat with mentors, if available, you pick up the phone and make some calls and perhaps you learn of other amazing people who did it successfully in an arena similar to yours. As with any new point in your development, new models arise that have laid the bread crumbs for you to learn from.

And that's the beauty of role models: they constantly change as you grow and change. Which means you have the opportunity to learn from different ones at different points in your own personal development.

Generally, learning involves not just classes, degrees and books, but also the knowledge that is gained from one another. The fiercely independent, maverick-style approach and the belief that you can go it alone does not bode well for success. Not one successful person in history became successful completely on their own. Everyone has had help — even if it's inspiration from someone they had only read about. When you open the book of their lives, you will find mentors and coaches, sages and muses, advisors and colleagues, spouses and friends that helped them along on their path to greatness. You may even find that they didn't personally know the people who helped them along and may not have even been alive when they were inspired by them.

In her book, *The Creative Habit: Learn It and Use It for Life*, the legendary American dancer and choreographer, Twyla

Tharp promotes the concept of role models and learning from those who come before you.

A life-long learner, Tharp would spend countless hours in the New York Public Library poring over books and photographs in the dance archives, soaking up photos of women pioneers in dance, among them Martha Graham, Doris Humphrey, Isadora Duncan and others.

"In a sense, I was apprenticing myself to these great women, much as Proust had to Ruskin and Chandler to Hemingway. A young friend of mine recently described an internship he was about to begin. He called the process "shadowing," following around a mentor and learning from him. That's what I was doing in the archives, shadowing my predecessors. This is how you earn your ancestry."

Just as Tharp did, by surrounding yourself with a community of people known to you or those you've admired from afar and learning from the vast cumulative knowledge available, you will rise to greatness in your own work and in your life.

Gotta Grow Your Mind... and Fast!

The use of role models — and, for that matter, anything that you learn in this book — will not help you one bit unless you get your beliefs and mindset on board. So it's time for some serious self-reflection. Ready?

Carol Dweck, a professor at Stanford University, is a world-renowned researcher on achievement, motivation and success. In her work, Dweck has found that there are two very distinct camps when it comes to mindset. One mindset, which she calls "fixed," is when an individual believes that her qualities are carved in stone. Everything is very black and white: traits are fixed in concrete, deep-seated and unchangeable; either you're smart or you're not, gifted or not; if you fail, you *are* a failure. Simple as that. The fixed mindset not only doesn't allow for much flexibility; it looks to blame others and outside forces for anything that may go wrong.

Dweck uses John McEnroe as the quintessential example of the fixed mindset. The way McEnroe saw it, he was supremely gifted — a natural and when things didn't go his way, he would blame everyone and everything on his failures. It is actually quite humorous the excuses he made when quite frankly he just hadn't practiced.

See if you recognize any of these beliefs:

- I am a certain kind of person and there is not much that can be changed about that.
- My intelligence is what I was born with and there is little I can do to change it.
- I can learn new things but I really can't improve the core intelligence that I was born with.
- I can learn to do things differently but the core of who I am isn't really changeable.
- If I'm really as smart or talented as I believe I am, this should come easy to me.

The fixed belief that your qualities are unchangeable creates an incredible urgency — a desperate need, even — to prove yourself over and over again. In the fixed mindset, you are constantly concerned with questions such as, "Will I fail or succeed?" "Will I appear dumb or smart?" or "Will I be accepted or rejected by others?"

Because of this need to constantly prove yourself — your character, your intelligence, your purpose for being on this planet — you seldom take risks that might place your basic traits in question.

You don't believe in effort because you firmly believe your talent is innate. In fact, effort is seen as something unsavory because that means you don't actually have the natural talent and smarts to begin with.

Now let's look at the other end of the spectrum: the much more flexible (and forgiving) growth mindset Those individuals who possess a growth mindset have a belief that the basic qualities of their personality can change, develop and cultivate through their own efforts. There is a strong belief that everyone can change and improve through education, learning, experience and the application of one's efforts. Potential is a driving force and challenges are sought in order to grow and expand.

Learning, being open to challenges, knowing that situations and setbacks don't define you — these are the baseline traits I want you to occupy before you proceed with the rest of this book. This is the foundation of the foundation — the first, substantial layer. Some of you may already be sporting the growth mindset (kudos to you, keep it up!); for others, this may be tough initial change to make. But it is a change you will *need* to make in order to prosper in business and life. Awareness is the first step. Once you are aware where your mindset lives on a daily basis, you can begin to move it to the camp where success, happiness and fulfillment lives and breathes, where mindsets thrive on growth and where you are focused on continuous improvement and purposeful progress.

One aspect of Dweck's research that I find truly inspiring is her observation that the growth mindset allows people to love what they're doing and to continue to love it even when faced with challenges, setbacks and difficulties. That's because those who possess a growth mindset value what they're doing regardless of the ultimate outcome.

Mindsets are simply beliefs, and beliefs are changeable.

So which do you choose. It is a choice, you know? You can either choose to be locked in a fixed mindset where you are constantly protecting your ego and avoiding anything that may challenge you, *or* you can embrace the vastness of the growth mindset where anything and everything is possible with effort and openness.

Not Competitors, but Collaborators, Colleagues, and Charming Examples

Women can be particularly vicious and ridiculously petty when it comes to other women, especially those we perceive as threats (women we classify as competitors). There are evolutionary, physiological, and psychological aspects at play here, but regardless of what's behind the behavior, we need to become more aware of how this competitive thought pattern and behavior sabotages our own efforts and diminishes the achievements of our sisters.

Coming back around to the fixed mindset, those of you who carry this heavy burden will also have a difficult time with others' successes. Fixed mindset folks often feel threatened by the success of others — especially those they see as their competitors. What results is a direct hit to your own ego: they're doing awesome, you're sucking it up. They're winning, you're losing. They're special and get it, whereas *you* clearly don't have what it takes.

People with a fixed mindset have an impossible time appreciating the efforts, successes and wins of other people and cannot find the lessons and inspiration that could impact their own work. Sadly, they also attribute their competitor's achievements to other factors which may or may not be true such as their network, their appearance, their connections, or that they just happen to be at the right place at the right time.

This thinking also comes from a scarcity standpoint— a belief that there is not enough to go around. A belief that if someone else has clients and customers that there is less for you. This isn't the case (and what a small, constricted way of viewing the world). From an energetic standpoint, the scarcity belief has a way of blocking the flow of one's own energy and, in turn, prevents the likelihood of attracting similar opportunities. After all, if you continue to believe that your competition is getting all the accolades, winning all the clients and making all the money, guess what: she will. And if you hold a belief that you can't measure up, that you just don't have what it takes to succeed and that you will never make a significant amount of money, then — you guessed it — you're right. Whether you believe in the Law of Attraction or not, begrudging others and being pissy towards your competitors is not only unbecoming and petty, it also will not help you succeed.

If you grew up in a competitive academic environment or played a lot of sports like I did, it is hard to turn this off. I understand how ingrained it can be in your personality. I find that I have to consciously turn the dial towards appreciating my competitors. I have learned to celebrate their success and now hum at a level of appreciation and gratitude (thankful that if they did it, this might open up doors for me too).

Have you ever stopped to consider that you can not only learn from the women who you believe are competitors but that they could also be your strongest allies and partners? Does this seem far fetched? It isn't.

How to get there from here? You can first thank your perceived rivals for the friendly competition which often fuels people to perform better and can challenge you to step further into your own greatness. In doing so, you may be surprised to find that your perceived competitors have something slightly different to offer your audience, and that, by coming together, you could potentially serve your customers better.

In *Creating Abundance: The A-Z Steps to a Richer Life*, Dr. Deepak Chopra suggests that exalting and celebrating in the success of others is the quickest way to your own success, and from personal experience, I have to agree. So find ways to view other women, women who may stir up feelings of insecurity in yourself, as not only potential colleagues, mentors and partners but also as potent guides to your success.

They're Everywhere, Once You Look

When I started my business, I didn't have many role models to speak of. To be perfectly honest, I didn't have any mentors or advisors to help me in the beginning stages when I needed it most. As much as I admire Martha Stewart and Oprah Winfrey, these ladies were not all that helpful when I was growing my email list or devising my five-year business plan. They are, what I fondly call, my stretch role models: women to be admired for the vastness of their empires and how prolific they have become in their work. I constantly remind myself that they have been around just a smidgen longer than I have been on the scene. Keeping this in mind, I nonetheless continue to keep my eye on them for models of mogul-level success, generosity and fierce dedication. They cause me to stretch my thinking that their greatness is possible for anyone with commitment, diligence and passion and hold a vision as to where I might be in my business twenty years from now.

However, in the beginning months and years of starting out on my own, I quickly realized that I needed more models that were within reach. I needed examples that resonated with the type of business I was building, my desire to write and publish, and my larger dreams of social change. I knew I had to actively seek them out. Most were not gracing the covers of business magazines or in the public eye, although some definitely were.

During this project, I spoke to amazing women across a broad array of industries and at different points in their businesses.

Some of the women I spoke to are in their twenties and rocking it in technology and brewing. Others are more seasoned business women, sharing stories of several successful companies they've grown, the changing landscape of women in business, and the decades of overcoming challenges. As I was introduced to more and more women, I realized that there are potential role models everywhere. They're in our communities, in our small towns, and members of our Chambers of Commerce. They are in our own industries and in industries we aren't even aware of. They are online, speaking at small and large venues and being interviewed by niche blogs and national magazines. They are women like you and me and they are just waiting to share their struggles and success with other women, if only they are asked.

There is a power that comes with surrounding yourself with others — your community and your tribe. Within your tribe, you have close confidants, peers, mentors, guides and role models. Unlike your family, your tribe can be chosen. So choose well. You can hand-select people who add significant value to your life and contribute to your growth at differing points in your career and at all levels. When mentors are not as readily available, you may have to search out women who you may not personally know or who you are not able to directly connect with — mentors *in absentia*, in other words, role models. Thankfully, with social media and the way in which our private lives are for open viewing (usually due in part to our own sharing), we are able to learn how women find success and balance in varying areas of their lives. You can even watch them in action thanks to YouTube, Vimeo, TedTalks and other outlets.

Stables Aren't Just for Horses

When you look at where you want to go and what it will take to get there, you discover quickly that there are several things you're hoping to glean from your prospective role models. So much so that one woman cannot possibly hold all these qualities.

Nor should she.

I advise that you pull together a full stable of prized models that you can draw on. For instance, you may be looking for inspiration and guidance on marketing, balancing family and business, and public speaking. You may look to role model Number One for how she propelled to fame through her strategic, innovative and streamlined marketing plan, while from role model Number Two you glean ideas on how she has managed three kids and launching a company at the same time. You know you could learn a lot about style and substance from role model Number Three just by watching footage of her presentations, speaking engagements and TED talks.

There may be women that you will admire for years while others may come and go as your business and life grows and changes. Each year or major milestone might see a new stable of role models.

For example, when I became a mom, my role models shifted dramatically. Don't get me wrong: I love my iconic role models as much as the next gal, but I needed help navigating my business with a newborn. My role models *du jour* never had children. I found that I ended up bitter and used excuses such as, "Well, she doesn't have children, so it was easy for her." I found that I often went to that nasty internal thinking when I found that my time and energy were squeezed dry. In the depths of my negative thinking, I realized I was using it both as an excuse for not getting certain things done and as an outlet for my generalized frustration and anger. I knew I needed to slow down a bit and figure more creative ways to organize my days. Patience has never been my strong suit, and when a little dependent person entered my life, I was faced with learning patience very quickly.

I soon realized that I needed different role models. I yearned for models of women managing the massive life change that happens when you have a child. Models who had both birthed a child and business at the same time. When I found others who I could learn from, there was a huge sense of relief. I also wasn't so bitter towards my previous role models from whom I still could learn a ton in areas that didn't involve family.

In my conversations with female entrepreneurs, one of the hottest and deeply problematic topic is work-family balance. In fact, many women I spoke to have created businesses to address just this problem. Every mom is trying to figure out solutions and strategies to integrate her family and business so neither suffers. This is one area where I personally can never get enough good ideas.

What many women are looking for in role models, besides understanding their obvious business success, is this understanding on how women balance or integrate family life with their business. It is tough raising kids and raising a business simultaneously, but women are doing it. Many women I interviewed noted that the women they admire are managing to juggle both with grace and they're taking a cue from their models on how to integrate the personal with the professional. For most women with children, the lines of business and family blur. You may bring work home or your home might be your place of work. You work evenings and weekends and between social engagements and soccer matches. Regardless of whether you have a family or not, there is no such thing as nine-to-five, clocking in and out. If you're not physically working on your business at all hours, you're often deep in thought about it. Women everywhere are figuring out what is working for them and there are lessons, strategies and tips that can be shared.

What areas are you hoping to improve? What are those big bold dreams that you're working towards and who are examples of women who have reached it?

Look to the iconic role models if you desire, but also know there are fantastic examples in your industries, communities and right next door. So be open to looking everywhere. To help you brainstorm some ideas of where to find not only role models but mentors, advisors and partners, see the end of this chapter for suggestions.

The Project (and What's Next)

In looking for role models for myself and in talking to other women who, when asked "who are your female entrepreneurial role models?" were shocked they could only name one or two, my passion project was born. I was not only curious about the concept of role models, but also what were the common traits, behaviors, and motivation that women entrepreneurs have in common. I had read many books on leadership qualities and most were grossly outdated as well as heavily focused on male business leaders and more traditional masculine traits.

I knew we were different.

I knew our motivations and how we defined success might be in sharp contrast to women in the corporate space or even from our mothers and grandmothers in the workforce before us.

And as I suspected, I was right.

So how, may you ask, did I figure this all out? It takes talking to a lot of women. When you aren't getting the answers you like and the deeper questions are not getting answered, it's a perfect time to reach out and talk to others.

And that is exactly what I did with the Role Models Wanted Project.

I love learning and studying up on topics that I'm passionate about, and I'm deeply passionate about women entrepreneurs. I believe we will be the mass force that will dramatically turn the current state of the world around. It is well known that women business owners give back more generously than our male business owner counterparts. Our love and gravitation towards community will be cornerstones of change. What better way to give back, then, than to provide jobs, monetarily contribute, pay for services and build companies with meaning and purpose.

In speaking to the women for this project, there was a clear trend in their motivation for starting a business: to help others in a meaningful way. It was so simple yet incredibly profound. That's how change starts.

My gift for you in this book is what I uncovered when I had the privilege to speak to a hundred women and research hundreds more. I have distilled it down so that you can focus, develop, nurture and strengthen these aspects that are probably already present in you.

These qualities, tactics and strategies can be learned. No one is born with the entrepreneurial gene that distinguishes them from others and guarantees that they will succeed. When talking with many women, they didn't have childhood dreams of running a business although there may have been a sign here or there.

When you speak to any entrepreneur, she will admit that there was a steep growth curve when she began, and one that continues to this day. Every day, she is met with challenges, opportunities to learn and pivot, and chances to grow beyond what she thought was possible. There is one important factor that you must keep in the forefront of your mind. This advice is wise to heed yet often overlooked: *You must maintain a fierce openness to learning.*

As Malcolm Gladwell has highlighted in his work, our culture rewards natural talent over hard work and effort. Don't fall prey to this notion. Know that if you are seeking greatness in your life and your life's work, it will require constant learning, tweaking and steadfastness to your bigger mission.

But isn't success so much sweeter when you give it everything?

Work doesn't need to *feel* like work, though, especially when the work you're doing is furthering your life's purpose and creating the life you desire.

Now that you have discovered ways to unearth models of success based on what you're moving towards in your business and life and you're maintaining a mindset focused on learning and growth, it is now time to learn what successful female entrepreneurs have in common. These common qualities provide a solid foundation on which to build your ideal business and life. Learning the mindset, traits and behaviors, and then both recognizing and developing them in yourself will be your constant — what you come back to time and again when challenges arise and obstacles try and stand in your way. Having this foundational piece in place, the tools available to tackle any challenge, and layering it with desirable role models to emulate and learn from makes the perfect recipe for delicious success.

Let's get started!

Places to Locate Potential Role Models and Mentors

1. **Business magazines**
   Examples: Forbes Magazine, Fortune Magazine, Entrepreneur Magazine. Don't just look at the Most Powerful Women lists or the Women to Watch lists, but also read the articles where they mention women-owned businesses and women leaders. Their online versions provide tons of great articles curated from independent writers and contributors.

2. **Specific industry/small business magazines**
   Examples: Fast Company, Inc Magazine, Wired

3. **Specific industry blogs and news sites**
   Example: Women2.0

4. **Women-entrepreneur focused blogs**
   Examples: Business Heroine, Glass Heel, The NextWomen, Claudia Chan.
   Many of these blogs highlight entrepreneurs who may be under the radar.

5. **Women business conferences**
   Examples: Spark & Hustle (Tory Johnson), Emerging Women Live (Chantal Pierrat), eWomen Network (Sandra Yancey), Shine (Ali Brown), S.H.E. Summit (Claudia Chan)

6. **Women writing on women in business**
   Example: Kathy Caprino, Contributor at *Forbes*, Moira Forbes, Contributor at *Forbes*, Geri Stengel, Contributor at *Forbes*

7. **Biographies on women business leaders and owners**
   Examples: *Lessons of a Lipstick Queen* by Poppy King, *Business As Unusual* by Anita Roddick, *By Invitation Only* by Alexis Maybank and Alexandra Wilkis Wilson, *The Widow Clicquot* by Tilar Mazzeo

8. **Local networking groups**
   Example: Chamber of Commerce, The Founding Moms (local chapters), Meetup

9. **Women-focused networking groups (online, nationally and local)**
   Examples: Savor the Success, Ladies Who Launch

10. **Women investing in women-founded companies**

PART TWO:
Modeling Success

*The savvy secrets of successful
female entrepreneurs and how you
too can become wildly successful.*

CHAPTER 3

Get Out of Your Own Way (Mindset)

"You were born with wings, why prefer to crawl through life?"

—Rumi

We can all agree that there is a certain madness that comes with wanting to start a business. It is not for those that will faint at the first sign of strife or struggle.

Mindset is the first crucial aspect we will look at. Mindset is simply our beliefs and our way of thinking about the world and ourselves. But there is nothing simple about either of these. That's because mindset is like a pair of glasses that can shade, distort, clarify or brighten our vision of the world. Your mindset can make or break you. And, a little known secret, it can make or break your business.

However, there is good news. The beauty of one's mindset is that it can be changed, and you can architect one that not only benefits your life, but also your business. As entrepreneurs, they're usually one in the same, right?

As women, *we* are our worst enemy. We may have great ideas for products, services and social causes, but we trip ourselves up with our uncertainty, fear, and self-doubt. We focus on these factors more than the factors that could actually enable us to be wildly successful. As Tony Robbins reminds us, "Focus on where you want to go, not on what you fear."

As we begin our look at what makes successful women entrepreneurs take risks, make substantial profits and create impact, our mindset is what will enable us to become successful as well. You need to de-clutter your mind of beliefs and thoughts that hold you back and quiet the internal naysayer that stops you from taking the necessary steps to move forward. You will get enough naysayers out in the world – which is usually a sign you're on to something – but this is no time to let the internal ones begin their destruction.

Once inspired, you need to make a conscious commitment to yourself. You are the only one who can commit to improving your life. While it's true that there are few things in life we have control over, we do have absolute control over our character, our mindset, and our behavior. Making a commitment to yourself and your personal growth is one of the most powerful business moves you can ever make.

The stories, suggestions and strategies in this book are not meant to only inspire you. You must be inspired *and* take purposeful and immediate action. Action can be in the form of tiny steps in the direction of starting a business, or large leaps jumping over obstacles that seem to be immovable. You must turn the positive feelings you ingest from the inspirational tidbits into movement that changes your life and propels you swiftly towards your dreams.

Be inspired. Commit. Act.

Face Fear

> "You gain strength, courage and confidence by every experience in which you really stop to look fear in the face. You are able to say to yourself, 'I have lived through this horror. I can take the next thing that comes along.' You must do the thing you think you cannot do."
>
> —Eleanor Roosevelt

Now is the time for you to stop and look fear in the face. This is the time to explore how it comes up for you and when. Here is the short list of some fears that may arise:

fear of failure
fear of the unknown
fear of success
fear of looking like a fool
fear of being rejecting
fear of appearing like a fraud
fear of public speaking
fear of overcommitting
fear of not being enough
fear of being selfish
fear there isn't enough for everyone
fear you don't have what it takes
fear of fear itself

It can all stop here – if you allow fear to win.

Just looking at this list makes my stomach churn. The catalogue of fears that can come up for you may be larger than *Vogue's* September Issue. And on some days, all these fears may decide to make an ensemble appearance just to bombard you into complete and utter paralysis. The flames of fear are fueled and stoked by our subconscious, the part of our deeper, internal functioning that is designed to protect us from harm. The subconscious often gets a bad rap for its trickery but it does have a solid purpose for its existence. The subconscious mind collects vast amounts of information from the world that the conscious mind cannot organize and retain and files it away for later use. It enables us to drive a car, while listening to music, talking on the phone and thinking about what to make for dinner, all at the same time. It keeps our internal systems running smoothly and automatically while we're busy living our lives.

Some scientists suggest that are mental functioning is made up of ninety percent from our subconscious and only ten percent from our conscious mind. That means that much of what we interpret about our world comes from our past experiences, memories, stories, interactions, traumas, and miscellaneous information we have gathered over our lifespan and is housed in our subconscious. Your subconscious mind accepts with is impressed upon it after it goes through your conscious filter. Let's say, as a child, you had a negative incident with a clown while attending the circus with your grandparents. You file away in your subconscious that clowns are scary, essentially placing a negative label on these brightly colored characters. Years go by and as an adult you still are uneasy around clowns and anyone for that matter who wears too much makeup. Clowns themselves are neither negative or positive but you have filed away in your subconscious that they are scary and unsafe. Your subconscious isn't analytical in the sense that it is going to argue with your conscious mind whether it's right or wrong or whether beliefs are true or false. It accepts how you've categorized and labeled the memory and looks to use this information to protect you (from devious clowns in this particular case) in the future.

In protecting us from physical and emotional harm (whether real or perceived), ridicule, and social ostracism, the subconscious also keeps us from taking chances, risks and asserting ourselves in ways that may be outside our comfort zone. When you realize that, in order to fulfill your dreams and life's purpose, you need to bypass the subconscious protective mechanism and dive into risky waters, it soon recognizes that its job is being phased out. Just like any other life-long employee banking on retiring at sixty-five year old with a fat pension, this employee, the fiercely dedicated subconscious, begins to resist. This is when crazy fears arise (*if I do this, I might lose all my friends and family*) and self-sabotaging behaviors manifest (you lose your voice before an important talk or you pick a fight with your investors on a minor aspect of a deal).

The subconscious is fighting dirty because its job — and survival — are on the line.

However, there is only one way to deal with the dense fog of fear and that is to recognize and name the fear and then transform it into something that ignites you. You see, most people allow their fearful thoughts to stop them. Often the best antidote for fear is action. By taking action, even if it's small micro steps in the beginning, you are reinforcing that it is safe to continue to do so by proving there is indeed nothing really to fear. The women I interviewed recognized their fears and went ahead and did what they wanted – they needed – to do to succeed.

Julie Azuma not only faced professional fears but also personal fears. Julie spent most of her career in the fashion industry but reached a certain point where one "was aged-out of fashion". She wasn't sure what her next steps would be in her career but soon that would all change after she adopted a beautiful little girl from Seoul, Korea in 1988. As the years past, she noticed that her daughter was missing important developmental milestones and specialists were not able to provide her with any answers. Still unable to talk, Miranda was six years old when she was finally diagnosed with severe autism. Julie and her husband sought out treatment options and turned to applied behavior analysis (ABA) a method for teaching language and social skills to autistic children.

Julie soon saw the benefits in ABA but she struggled to find appropriate flash cards and other education tools to complement this approach. She quickly realized that there was a need in the marketplace for such tools and began searching out suitable materials and distributors to source and create such products. She approached three different people to partner with and each of them told her it was not a viable business. One person even called her idea "dumb". She never imagine starting a business of her own let alone launching one with a child who needed significant care. Julie shared, "I started with great support from friends but most didn't believe there would be a market." However in 1995 she took the leap regardless of her own fear. She started Different Roads to Learning, a company that sells products such as books, flashcards, and other tools to help parents with autistic children. Today the company has over five hundred products available through it's online store and more than two million in sales. "Everyone has a fear of failure, but you have to have the courage to keep going," Julie shared. Thankfully she kept going and overcame her own fears to provide a much-needed service to families everywhere dealing with autism.

I used to look at highly successful people and think that they were fearless, that they were not afraid of anything or anyone. In order for them to scale the heights that I admired, they couldn't be riddled with fearful thoughts, insecurity or uncertainty. The fact is, successful people are no different than you and I. They do have fears, but the difference is that they don't let them stop them from moving forward and chasing after their dreams. If anything, they move towards what frightens them. They know that by pushing themselves outside their comfort zone, this is where the magic will be found, where the pieces of their business all fall into place, and where they were born to play.

Fears can be naughty friends and trickier foes. Similar to your enemies, you should keep them close — but only close enough to recognize their cunningness and yet far enough aside to march past them towards your future. By keeping a keen eye on what scares you and what pushes certain buttons, you will discover the quickest path to your success. It's an excellent opportunity for personal growth.

What can you learn from fear, and what are your fears telling you? While you have your flashlight poised to shine a light on fears it's a great time to ask them, "What are you trying to tell me?" Probe further and inquire "Why now?" In his brilliant book, *The War of Art*, Steven Pressfield stresses, "The more scared we are of a work or calling, the more sure we can be that we have to do it." He examines and dissects why we resist doing the work that we really want to do and why we can find thousands of reasons why we can't do, have or be what we desire. He particularly describes how tricky this resistance, which essentially is based in fear, can be although it's a sign of where you ought to traverse. However when you realize that you are going to be facing your fears and that they're a flashing neon sign pointing you in the direction of your dream, calling, and purpose, you soon realize you are, in fact, on the right path.

Embrace Failure

The fear that comes up most often for anyone starting a business is the fear of failure. It is what keeps most people comfortably in their corporate jobs, never even tiptoeing onto their brighter paths. People dish out failure rates anytime you talk about starting a business and articles, books, organizations, and governmental statistics illustrate the point. They can be sobering if you chose to believe them, but don't let the numbers keep you from joining the party. You are different. You are taking the steps to give yourself the best chance at success. What you don't often see in these statistics are whether the entrepreneur went on to build a successful company after learning lessons from the first venture. You don't see what they may have learned from the experience or the reasonings behind closing the business. Regardless of the circumstances, failure isn't something to avoid. It is actually something to embrace – regularly, and in small doses.

Sara Blakely, founder of Spanx, is the world's youngest self-made female billionaire. She knows a thing or two about failure. In an interview with *Forbes* magazine she shared, "My dad encouraged us to fail. Growing up, he would ask us what we failed at that week. If we didn't have something, he would be disappointed. It changed my mindset at an early age that failure is not the outcome, failure is not trying. Don't be afraid to fail."

Sara had some epic and humorous failures on her ascent to the top, including two years of her product being flat-out rejected, as well as a funny incident on international television. In an interview with the BBC, she repeatedly kept describing her product by saying, "It smoothes and separates your fanny." In the UK, "fanny" doesn't refer to one's bottom. It actually refers to a woman's vagina. Can you imagine the horror to find that out in the middle of an interview on international television? But she rolled with it. The first time I read her quote on failure was a huge turning point for me. I knew I needed to approach failure in a different way. Failure is not to be avoided; it is something to consistently learn from and to whole-heartedly embrace, knowing that you've taken chances in your life. Each and every failure is a seed of insight and opportunity.

Quite frankly, if you're not stumbling a bit or experiencing moments of failure than you're not taking big enough risks. We'll talk more about risks in Chapter 5 when it comes to behavior of successful women. Unfortunately some people equate the act of failing with being identified as a failure. The actions you've taken and the results do not define who you are; they're merely road signs indicating you may need to take a different route.

Failure and taking big risks hasn't stopped Christiane Lemieux, founder of design and lifestyle company, Dwell Studios. She started her business without a business plan (she does not advise this) and not knowing what a PO was and through lots of learning (which she loves) has built a hugely successful company that was recently acquired by Wayfair. com. She believes that "Some of your greatest lessons are in the failures." She strongly advocates that life is an adventure and the sum total of all your experiences. "Being an entrepreneur is all about taking risks and not being afraid of failure. There is a poetry in the journey," Christiane shared.

The day I spoke with Christiane she was preparing to jet off with fellow powerhouse entrepreneur Mariam Naficy to Haiti to do charitable work. The two are good friends and board members of the organization Every Mother Counts which is a non-profit campaign to end preventable deaths caused by pregnancy and childbirth around the world.

Mariam, founder of Minted has had her share of success and challenging moments. When she was still in her 20s, she sold her company Eve.com, an online cosmetic retailers, for $110 million. Things didn't go nearly as smoothly when she launched Minted in 2008. The press and one prominent Stanford business professor were skeptical that you could sell paper products online and, to make matters worse, Minted had only one sale in the first month. Coming off the heals of such a well-publicized success, she felt the pressure to make this company just as successful. Her investor's money and her reputation were on the line. At one point, she seriously considered giving the investors back their money and walking away. She thought she had "a lemon on her hands." After weighing her options, she realized she had already spent some of her investor's money and decided to figure out a way to turn things around. In her words, she needed to "squeeze lemonade out of this lemon."

Mariam intelligently looked at what was working and what was not and found a gem in one aspect of her business where the analytics showed some success. She revamped the company to focus on that one particular element and marched forward. When it comes to business and failure, you need to "Steel yourself for a lot of rejection and a lot of criticism of your idea. You have to be prepared as a successful entrepreneur not to care what other people think about you, except your customers. That is the only person you actually should care about," she shared in an interview on TechCrunch. As a result of listening to her customers and learning from daily failures and mistakes, she has taken what some would have tossed and has made a successful enterprise out of it.

Challenge: Managing and Overcoming Fear

What scares you?

1. List out every fear you have about starting or growing your business. This may require a few sheets of paper, which is okay. It's important to first recognize what is bubbling under the surface and shine a light on the internal obstacles that could hold you back.

2. Once you've listed them out, ask yourself, "Why do I believe that this is real and possible?" Are there circumstances in the past that didn't go well and that you're afraid of repeating? Are their childhood memories that pop up for you as you write these down? Flesh those out, too and write them down.

3. Now, next to each item you've listed, indicate the likelihood in a percentage of that fearful event actually happening. Often when we're forced to put a number to our exaggerated beliefs, we realize how unlikely it is that it will occur.

4. With each item, it's time to turn around your beliefs about them. Restate your fearful inner talk as a positive statement. For example: "I'm so afraid that my business will be a huge failure."

    Restate it: "I'm committed to making my business a success and I'm confident I will do everything in my power to do so."

    Bonus: Recall any past moments, situations or projects where your failed. Did something positive come out of the it? Did the event(s) steer your life in a different direction? How would your life be different had you succeeded? What did you learn from the event and did it bettered your life?

Foster Optimism

> "A pessimist sees the difficulty in every opportunity;
> an optimist sees the opportunity in every difficulty."
> —Winston Churchill

Optimism has been given a bad rap. The brooding, cynical, sarcastic realist, à la Woody Allen, has been *en vogue* for many years until the recent happiness movement replaced this darker side with a bright cheerfulness that many of us had been desperately craving. And thank goodness. Researchers believe that pessimism is actually a survival mechanism that dates back to prehistoric times. Although we may have outgrown the basic need for this fight-or-flight function, our brains still use pessimism to help us in threatening or stressful situations.

How does optimism play into business success, though? In fact, being all sunshine and flowers can make you a stronger entrepreneur. One of the main traits seen time and again in powerful leaders at all levels is positive framing. It should be no surprise that to manage the roller coaster that is running your own business, you have to keep an outlook that looks for the silver lining in situations. But it goes beyond just having a rose-colored perspective. It is also about seeing things for the way they are and taking the facts as facts rather than spinning stories that are not true or — for that matter — useful. In his book *Learned Optimism*, Martin Seligman describes three lenses of optimism that people use to view a particular situation:

Permanence: Optimists see positive situations as permanent and negative situations as fleeting.
Pervasiveness: Optimists see positive situations as pervasive while negative situations are simply isolated incidences.
Personal: Optimists see situations as in their control and view negative situations as external events out of their control.

By knowing how you tend to view situations, you will cultivate and maintain a positive outlook while preventing yourself from diving into a downward spiral of negativity and pessimism.

People who frame things in a positive light don't let negative feelings paint their reality in a negative way. They see things for what they are and learn from them. They understand that they're in control of their future and can influence future outcomes, learn, and grow.

Stella Grizont, founder of WOOPAAH and one of the first two hundred people to earn a Masters in Applied Positive Psychology from the University of Pennsylvania believes that entrepreneurs already come to the table optimistic, fairly delusional (in the best sense of the word) and with a strong belief in themselves. She believes it's deeper than just being optimistic and looking simply on the bright side. According to Stella what is most important is a belief in your vision and seeing ways to maneuver difficult situations and challenges. While a leader within the Ladies Who Launch organization she worked with thousands of women helping them maintain a positive frame by seeing the possibilities, taking the next step and taking account of one's previous successes. This valuable tool of reframing situations, challenges and obstacles is a skill that can take you far.

Not only do entrepreneurial women have a set of beliefs that they can control their destiny and influence the outcomes but most of these women started a business because they wanted more control of their lives. That was a significant driver for launching on their own.

There is a lot of overlap between the concept of learned optimism that comes out of the positive psychology community and Carol Dweck's work on growth mindset.

Both concepts and ways of viewing the world lead to success not only in your professional life, but in all areas of your personal life.

Spotlight: Gail Gibson Cmiel On Optimism

Gail has always managed to keep a positive attitude even when the cards were stacked against her. She grew up in Southern Illinois in a conservative town. She was one of only four girls out of her high school class to attend college. She reminded me that when she was younger, "there were no roles for women other than mother, nurse or school teacher." She always felt that it was important to go against the grain and take a different direction in life. She received her Masters in Social Work and began working with the geriatric community with a particular interest in the prison population. After becoming dismayed at how the United Way was run (the company her husband worked for donated money to the organization), she began writing a business plan on how she could meet the needs of the people better than what she saw being accomplished by the United Way. She pitched her business plan to a therapist she knew who thought it was a great idea and her first company was born.

Gail's company was growing when her husband landed a political job in Washington D.C. This was in the early 1980s and it wasn't typical for spouses to live in two cities. She dissolved her partnership and sold all of their belongings (even gave their dog away) and off to D.C. the pair went. Given her experience, she interviewed with the largest employee assistance agencies and left each interview thinking "Holy crap, I can do this one thousand times better than these people with one hand tied behind my back."

She had a moment that so many entrepreneurs have where they realize that they are meant to create their own business. The seed was planted. She headed home to share in her epiphany only to be met with a conflicting epiphany from her husband. Her husband decided he no longer wanted to be married and in fact was already involved with someone else.

News like this can be crushing but Gail took it in stride and immediately went into figuring out how she was going to live and survive. She had no job, no place to live and was sharing a car with her husband. She left the house that day and went to the Economic Development Corp. and did an assessment of businesses she wanted to launch. Less than fifty hours after the conversation with her husband she found a condo, signed a lease, moved out and secured the use of a conference room in an office complex to start her company. She had to give up the car and walked two miles each way everyday (sidewalks had yet to be added to the streets) to her "office". She grew her company, Employment Assistance Services Corp into one of the most successful EAP (employee assistance programs) in the country which she sold in 1997 to The Menninger Foundation. She had traveled frequently between her offices in Philadelphia, Virginia, Dallas and Southern California and had over four hundred employees and three thousand contractors. She retired in 2005 and now mentors business owners who are finding they are having partnership issues and companies that have potential buyers knocking on their door. Both areas that she has had a lot of experience in.

Gail faced many challenges along her journey but none stopped her from pursuing her passion. Her optimistic attitude which she also finds is invaluable when working with large teams has enabled her to live exactly the life she wanted.

Optimism is contagious and a strong leader leads from a positive frame. Not only does this optimism serve you well during challenges times, but it can also rally your team and customers. A positive frame is also crucial when you're trying to tackle a new industry or when you're challenging a traditionally conservative industry or the status quo.

Like so many other entrepreneurs, Lily Szajnberg, founder of GAGE, believes that optimism is a crucial quality for business owners. GAGE is a startup that uses 3D cameras and face-tracking to provide a cheap, accessible way to do gait assessment tests and gesture evaluations all from the comfort of the patient's home. Lily has bigger dreams for her startup though. She visualizes paving the way for a better model for healthcare startups and for the healthcare system as a whole. That's one tall order. "I've adopted a Pollyanna-in-hell mindset," Lily said with a chuckle. It's a quality she learned from her first role model: her mom. Lily's mom was a single parent raising two girls on a Kindergartner teacher's salary. "She has always been so optimistic and helps you sort out something without ever injecting her opinion," she noted. This optimistic outlook will serve her well as she challenges and changes the behemoth that is the U.S. healthcare system.

Challenge: Become a Pollyanna

You don't need to skip around staring up at the clouds, but you can work on being a more optimistic person. In his book, *Flourish*, Martin Seligman notes that positive emotions can be turned up each day by a simple bedtime ritual. He suggests that each evening you write down three things that went well for you that day, and why. That way, instead of ruminating about your day and what you didn't accomplish or what didn't go well, you can unwind by focusing on the positive aspects of your day.

Another simple exercise that many women I spoke to incorporate into their daily routine is keeping a gratitude journal. At the end of each day, you simply jot down three to five things that you are grateful for that day. It's a lovely way to fall into a peaceful slumber.

Optimism is contagious so take stock of the people around you. If you're finding that you have a lot of Negative Nelly's around, it may be time to do some spring cleaning. You may have to distance yourself from the negativity or remove yourself altogether.

> Also, don't underestimate the impact that media has on your outlook. If you are consuming vast amounts of negative information in the form of news and media, you may be inadvertently darkening your perspective of the world. It may be time for a media detox until you can clear up those dark cloudy skies of your mind.

Fiercely Commit

"We can do anything we want as long as we stick to it long enough."

—Helen Keller

One glaring quality that came up with all the women I interviewed is a fierce commitment to what they are doing and the impact they want to have on the lives of their employees, customers, community and the world. Commitment is the jet fuel that keeps people going when all the signs say to quit. It is the internal contract they have made with themselves that they're all in. It may not be the sexiest aspect of success, and it's likely you'll find your commitment challenged every time you're overwhelmed, when you're doing tasks you dislike, and especially during challenging times. Successful women work at a level of rabid persistence that only comes from a deep commitment to their passion, their purpose, their work, and the impact it has on others.

Committing to a project or a business can be a scary proposition. It can stir up all the fears we have already discussed. What I found with the women I studied and interviewed is that their commitment ran at such a deep level that fear and self-doubt didn't stand a chance at keeping them down.

Your every success hinges on just how committed you are, and without this commitment you are only using half your power to reach your most precious goals — whatever they may be. Just as you'd commit to your partner, to a social cause, or to a healthy lifestyle, you need to determine if what you're undergoing deserves this level of commitment. And if the answer is yes, then dive in.

Commitment need not be overly rigid. It's important to stay committed to your decision to dive in, to your larger why and to your bigger mission but stay always flexible in your approach and how life unfolds. There are too many uncertain factors that can and will arise. Commit but stay open. Commit but allow for pivots when necessary. Commit but be open to shifting directions. Commit to your mission, vision, and purpose but be flexible in the execution.

Commitment is a practice in many ways. Especially when you may be going against the norm as one often does when they've started their own business. Your family and friends may not understand the widget you've created or the service you're providing, but they will understand and feel the commitment you've made to bringing it into the world. That commitment is what rallies together your team and piques the interest of investors. It is also what will draw in your most loyal fans and customers because they feel your devotion that you're all in.

When Michelle Long decided she wanted to open a wellness and yoga retreat specifically for moms, she was committed to finding the perfect space. She knew that to create the setting she envision, it had to feel like a home away from home where tired moms could recharge and connect. It took her two years to locate the ideal place. Michelle was a first time business owner and people were not keen on leasing space to a new and unproven business concept. When she found the location that was exactly what she envisioned she was saddened to be turned down. She knew in her heart she had to fight for it. She found out the building owner was an elderly woman and decided to write a heartfelt letter to her directly. The letter made an impression and they leased her the space. "I tried to give up many times but there is a force in me – it's huge – a force to put my soul's work out there and to never give up," said Michelle.

As challenges arise, you have to re-commit to your commitment. You may have to recommit daily — especially when you're in the start-up phase. You have to focus on what will drive your mission and business forward, eliminate distractions, and sift through what is necessary and what is just fluff. You may even have to assess relationships to determine whether they fit into your new way of being and living. For many of the women I interviewed, it was necessary to let go of toxic people who were draining them of energy and knocking them off course. This singleness of focus might sound pathological, but when your passion is on the line — and if that passion is entwined with your life's purpose — it will be the best commitment you've ever made to yourself.

Challenge: Commitment

What are you willing to commit to?
You can take baby steps with your commitment to warm-up. Perhaps you want to just put a toe in the water and commit to becoming clearer on your business purpose and big idea. Maybe you will commit to researching different distributors, Internet providers, or textile options this week.

Ponder the following questions and write down what you will commit to:

What commitment am I making to myself?
What commitment am I making to my business?
What commitment am I making to my customers or potential customers?
What can I commit to this month to push my business one step forward?
What can I commit to this week to move my business forward?
What can I commit to today that will keep me moving forward?

Spotlight: Kellee Khalil On Committing to the One

When you talk about weddings and marriage, commitment is the name of the game. When you talk to Kellee Khalil you realize her commitment to starting her own business was there long before she decided to tackle the ninety billion dollar a year wedding industry.

Kellee's dad came to the U.S. with only $27 in his pocket and started and grew a business from the ground up. He instilled the importance of working hard, tenacity and the value of money in all five of his kids. Kellee always knew she wanted to start her own company and studied entrepreneurism while at University of Southern California. After college and still unclear on the type of business to launch, she took a job in finance. She disliked the job but knew that she could learn a lot and make good money. She thoughtfully and strategically saved seventy five thousand dollars by living within her means and socking everything else away.

After years of making four hundred sales calls a day and being passed over for promotions, she decided it was time to move on. Her sister had built her own PR firm that catered to the wedding industry. Kellee decided to work with her to grow the company's presence on the East Coast. She loved the wedding industry with all its beauty and color. It suited her much more than her previous work environment. She also realized while helping to plan her sister's wedding that there was clearly something missing in the wedding industry and that was a one-stop search engine and cloud scrapbook just for wedding ideas and products. The idea just wouldn't leave her and she realized that this was *the one*.

With the savings she had accumulated, she invested in creating the first version of Lover.ly before eventually attracting more money from angel investors. She is fully committed to making her idea work even when others in the technology community don't understand her. "I'm not a tech person so people don't take us as a serious technology company. Most male investors don't understand the industry and don't see the real need." She isn't letting that phase her. After launching on Valentine's Day in 2012 she has grown the company to thirteen employees and has nearly three million users across its site and blogger network. Those users view around forty million images a month. She is also committed to her brand and preserving authenticity. When she began approaching venture firms, she was once advised to tone down her lipstick and ditch her heels. For an instant, she considered trading in her signature bright pink hues and high heels for bland neutral shades and a grey suit. However, she realized that in subduing her signature style she would not be representing the company and her target audience. "This is my personal brand, I'm not wearing a hoodie," she said with a laugh. She is committed to building trust through being totally authentically Kellee – pink lipstick, stilettos and all.

Figure It Out

"We'll never survive!"
"Nonsense. You're only saying that because no one ever has."
—William Goldman, *The Princess Bride*

No one who launches a business knows everything that they need to know to begin. Even if someone has an MBA, it doesn't mean that she will know how to hire the right people for her team, understand how to ship her product overseas, or will know her way around a manufacturing floor. For many women, just learning the financial aspects of running a business was a challenge that needed to be addressed immediately.

Known as one of the top female chefs in the country, Traci Des Jardins, is a classically trained chef and has been trained by some of the best chefs and restaurateurs in the world. When it came time to launch her own restaurant Jardinière in San Francisco in 1997 and as she expanded her restaurant empire, raising money was her biggest challenge. She had no formal training in business and leaned on a business partner to help her figure it out. "One has to have a basic understanding of all aspects of the business so that oversight is possible," she shared. Similar to the restaurant environment, business as Traci puts it is an "evolve or die" way of life. One important aspect she has discovered along the way is that you cannot micromanage your way to understanding the business either. You need to have trust in that the team you hire is doing good work.

As an entrepreneur and business owner you have to embrace the learning process because it is constant. You may be doing tasks that you never thought you'd be doing but, especially in the early stages out of necessity, you take them on.

Kimberly Wilson started her business out of her living room. In 1999, she offered yoga classes out of her tiny apartment in Washington, D.C. She eventually outgrew her space and started opening studios in town. She also launched an eco-fashion line, created a foundation to give back to causes she believes in and wrote three books all while pursuing her Master's degree in Social Work. What she found the most challenging when starting out was how difficult it was to focus on the creative aspect of her business – the part she loves. Like most entrepreneurs, you're "forced to to be the jack of all trades and wear all the hats yourself" she reminisced. When she started she was in her mid 20s and her business was all-consuming. "On Friday nights when everyone else was out, I was recoding my website," she recalled. She gave everything she had to her yoga studios and the business and years later it has definitely paid off. Her studio, Tranquil Space, was named among the top 25 yoga studios in the world by Travel + Leisure, she leads retreats globally and generously gives back to animal rights organizations through her foundation.

Both Traci and Kimberly value that they had to learn different aspects of their business because they are better equipped to understand the value of different roles, what it takes to be successful and are better able to lead those who take on that function. It has served them both well as they grow their businesses and expand their reach.

Entrepreneurs are natural problem-solvers. The mere fact that they're solving a problem or providing a solution in the form of a product or service is a testament to this. But it goes even further as their problem solving skills are tested on an almost daily basis. Just because they don't know how to do something doesn't stop them from pursuing their dreams and getting the job done. Nearly all the women I interviewed noted that one of the largest challenges they faced was that they didn't know exactly what they were doing. But, they overcame the challenge by simply figuring it out.

In her book *Business as Unusual*, Anita Roddick, the founder of The Body Shop shared that entrepreneurs have "a covert understanding that you don't have to know *how* to do something. Skill or money isn't the answer for the entrepreneur, it is knowledge: from books, observing and asking." Roddick, who passed away 2007 was also an environmentalist and a human rights activist and was a pioneer in shaping ethical consumerism. She gives several examples throughout her book on how she made things work. For instance, everyone assumes that the interior dark green paint on the walls of The Body Shop stores was a reflection of being a "green" company. When she launched her first store in 1976, "green" was not a metaphor for the environmental movement. She simply used dark green because it was the only color that would cover up all the damp patches on the walls. Also, the concept of using reusable bottles was purely because she couldn't afford to purchase enough to keep them in stock. "Every element of our success was really down to the fact that I had no money," Roddick writes.

The ability to be creative in solving problems and looking for solutions where others might not look, is a valuable quality in an entrepreneur. As with Roddick, some of her early decisions were not necessarily about being eco-friendly, she was simply looking for ideas to make her business work on limited resources.

Lori Saitz knows a thing or two about figuring things out. In the early days of her company, Zen Rabbit, she realized that to grow her baking company she needed to find a contract baking partner rather than baking out of church kitchen. She located an amazing baker and was thrilled about starting the relationship. Just six months in, she was the proud recipient of her biggest cookie order to date. She was on top of the world when tragedy struck. The weekend that the order was to be processed the baker was killed in a car crash. Lori was saddened as she took an instant liking to the man, but it also left Lori pressed for time if she was to honor her commitment. Frantic, she scurried around to find someone who could fill the order to her specific needs. It wasn't easy, but she did what she needed to do. She figured it out instead of throwing in the towel which would have been easy to do under the circumstances. As Lori remembers, "There were so many points where I just wanted to say 'I'm done,' but true entrepreneurs always think the real success is just around the corner." She didn't let this one early setback destroy her resolve or her business dreams. Her company is still going strong after ten years and she is grateful for every challenge and learning experience along the way.

The tendency to look for creative solutions is one that you may have never noticed in yourself before, but I'm willing to bet it is there. You are probably using it in other areas of your life, like dealing with friends and family or when you cook, travel or shop, and you are not even aware of it. It's a quality that will launch you from where you are to where you want to be and will get you out of sticky messes as well.

For solopreneurs or women who are launching a business from their home office, the notion of *figuring it out* is a necessity. If you're starting out as a one-woman show, there is a tremendous learning curve just to get to a point where you can begin collecting money for your product or service. You have to figure out how to build a website (or find someone who can), build your audience, become a superstar in the social media space, market, sell, ship, and account for every detail. It's no small undertaking, and each day is a lesson in perseverance and patience.

For those of you who are building larger companies, you may have to learn about fundraising, commercial leasing, managing significantly-sized teams, managing investor expectations, human resources, and corporate governance. Either large or small, solo or massive, you constantly are pushed to figure out what to do and how to grow for the future.

This quality of figuring things out is built into Sarah Hernholm's non-profit Whatever It Takes. The title says it all. Sarah's path to the non-profit world was an atypical one. She started out in Hollywood working in TV and film. She thought she had reached the levels of success she desired only to find that she was unhappy. While on a plane from New York back to the West Coast after wrapping up filming *Elf*, she stared out at the black abyss and realized that the work she was doing didn't make her happy. In fact, it was leaving her depleted and miserable. She decided to leave Hollywood for San Francisco and in an unlikely career transition became a preschool teacher.

At the time she was going through a break up but as she shared, "I had to show up everyday. I had ten kids under four years old and they need you to show up." This was a powerful lesson for her and she began showing up larger for herself as well. She loved teaching and realized it is truly her calling.

She returned home to San Diego to get her teaching credential and then began teaching elementary school. She soon discovered that the kids had no interest in doing their homework and had little guidance at home to fulfill basic academic requirements. Shocked and dismayed, she created a banner that she put up in the classroom that read "Whatever It Takes." It was a motto for the kids. She starting teaching the kids that regardless of what was happening at home they needed to start showing up for themselves. She began teaching them resourcefulness and the importance of giving back. After Hurricane Katrina, the kids wanted to do something to help. She didn't impose on them what they could do to raise money, she left it up to them. She told them "You have to figure out how to help" and they did by doing chores around their neighborhoods to raise money and book drives to replenish the school books lost in the storm. It was great for their self-esteem and confidence.

Even though her work was changing the lives of the children in her classroom, the administration wasn't fond of how she was outshining tenured teachers and she was let go. This didn't stop Sarah. She realized the importance of service-oriented after school programs and quickly launched her non-profit that now focuses primarily on high school age kids. Whatever It Takes teaches kids to be leaders and social entrepreneurs. She instills in them that anything can be figured out. As she shared about her own experience starting a company, "I have Google, I can figure it out. I can get guidance and surround myself with people smarter than me." Nothing can stop Sarah from pursuing her dreams of taking her program to every state in the U.S. and eventually launching programs internationally. She has wisely created a "Mini Board: A meeting of the minds" as she calls her advisors who she bounces ideas off of and receives invaluable advice from.

As seen in the kids that Sarah works with, the added benefit of constantly being resourceful is its impact on one's confidence. The same goes for you as an entrepreneur. After all, nothing builds your confidence and self-esteem faster than overcoming challenges you face along the way. By maintaining a mindset and a belief that everything can be figured out, you are setting yourself up for increased confidence, higher levels of self-esteem and notable business success. That sounds like an awesome trifecta to me.

Challenge: Figuring It Out

What can you do today to make a step forward in your business by figuring something out that has been perplexing you?

What if you could pick up the phone and simply ask someone for guidance? Who would you call? (You don't have to know them – yet.)

What if you Googled it and allotted one hour researching and deciding upon a solution? What's stopping you from finding a solution? Dig deep on this one.

What does it mean if you found a solution to a specific issue?

Might it mean that you have to move forward?

Does it mean you may be taking bigger risks?

Does it mean you may be traveling out of your comfort zone?

Spotlight: Rachel Brown On Passion, Commitment and a Little Bit of Magic

Rachel had tried many different businesses through the years but was never entirely happy with any of them. When she finally discovered what her next business would be – mixing her love of jewelry and the Kabbalah – she knew she had to make it happen. "I felt that the pain would be stronger not doing this than doing it and failing," Rachel shared during our interview. After being denied for several traditional bank loans and having several purchasing promises revoked, she was frustrated yet determined. "Whenever I was frustrated, I'd go to Barney's. I would look at the jewelry case and know that I could do this and do it more powerfully. I couldn't live with myself if I didn't do it."

She knew she needed a few solid pieces to get started. In an attempt to get away, she and her boyfriend had planned to go to New Jersey for the weekend. Her boyfriend's sister told her that her brother was extremely lucky and maybe she could win some of her start-up money. She thought, "why not," and ascended on the Baccarat table with a mission. Rachel came away that weekend with not only the $3,000 she needed to start her business, but also won three pairs of Jimmy Choo's.

But she didn't stop there. Persistence paid off for Rachel when she was introduced by a close friend to someone in Donna Karan's organization. This was her dream opportunity since Karan is also into Jewish mysticism. After the initial introduction, Rachel emailed the contact and asked if Karan would accept one of her pieces as a gift. She agreed to the gift. After the appropriate amount of time, Rachel sent a friendly note asking for feedback. A series of emails ensued. "I just want feedback that she got it," she implored. After exchanges with layers of assistants and assistants of assistants, she finally received word that the piece was in Donna Karan's personal closet. Rachel was pleased, but not entirely satisfied with this.

She didn't want her beloved (and expensive) piece laying in the bottom of a closet somewhere. The assistant trying to smooth over the situation said she would just mail back the gold cuff to Rachel. Disappointed and frustrated, Rachel insisted that she would personally pick it up.

Three days later she got a call that Donna Karan had planned to wear the piece for a story that was being done on her at Urban Zen for US Weekly (which was probably why it was her in personal closet). Rachel was elated and had it hand-delivered by the friend who made the initial introduction. She carefully wrapped it and included a heartfelt note sharing how the piece was inspired by Karan's early jewelry collaboration with the famous jewelry designer and sculptor Robert Lee Morris. When Karan opened it and read the letter, she teared up. She was so excited to receive the piece (again) and even further moved that the piece was inspired by Karan's early foray into jewelry.

Many times along Rachel's journey she could have thrown her hands up and retreated. But her commitment to her business fuels her to continue producing beautiful pieces that will be loved by others as much as she loves them.

Your mindset and beliefs about yourself and your world are completely in your hands. You can choose to face your fears, maintain an optimistic outlook, commit to your mission, and create an attitude that you can figure anything out. You can either get your beliefs on board with your dreams in order to move swiftly forward, or you can let false beliefs, outdated thoughts of yourself, or past events hold you back. Again, it's your choice. It's all up to you.

Inspiration Library

Music
Lose Yourself by Eminen
Roar by Katy Perry
Shake It Out by Florence + the Machine
Don't Stop Believin' by Journey

Movies
The Intouchables
Along Came Polly
The King's Speech
Yes Man

Books
Mindset: The New Psychology of Success by Carol Dweck
The Creative Habit: Learn It and Use It for Life by Twyla Tharpe
The Big Leap: Conquer Your Hidden Fear and Take Life to the Next Level by Gay Hendricks
Turning Pro: Tap You Inner Power and Create Your Life's Work by Steven Pressfield
Flourish: A Visionary New Understanding of Happiness and Well-being by Martin Seligman

CHAPTER 4

Get Clear (Motivation)

> "Be of good cheer. Do not think of today's failures, but of the success that may come tomorrow. You have set yourselves a difficult task, but you will succeed if you persevere; and you will find a joy in overcoming obstacles. Remember, no effort that we make to attain something beautiful is ever lost."
> —Helen Keller

When I was living in both San Francisco and New York City in my late 20s and early 30s, there was hardly a Sunday morning that I didn't wake up with some shade of hungover. In San Francisco, I was single, and Saturday nights meant more than just hanging out with friends; it meant covertly seeking out potential boyfriend material as well. When I luckily found him, he and I moved to New York City, where we lived the big city life full of adventures, delicious meals, great wine and new friends. Those Sunday mornings were always rough, and luckily, in New York, breakfast and coffee were a quick phone call away. Beside an entire day wasted lounging about the apartment, my head always felt thick with a haze that made my thoughts muddled. I felt like I was behind a think veil that no amount of water, coffee, vitamins, food or sleep could penetrate. When the regular partying life was replaced with early sobering mornings with a toddler, the haze would reappear from time to time. This time it wasn't alcohol induced, nor was it due to sleep deprivation or not the adequate amount of caffeine.

At different points in my business and in the writing of this book, I would fall into a state that I could only compare to being hungover. My thinking became fuzzy, I was unfocused, the world seemed confusing and my ideas were like faint whispers in the back of my head. The ideas did not connect, nor did they make sense. I wanted to yell, "What the hell are you saying back there? What's going on? What am I suppose to do next?" But, what I realized very quickly is that I was lacking clarity. The ability to see clearly why I was doing what I was doing and what my overall strategy was to move my life and business forward. I realized that my fog and mild discontent were due to my ill-defined, although present, drive to do something bigger. I wasn't clear as to the direction of my purpose and my business, and, therefore my life.

Getting clear is not about knowing the exact direction your life is heading or plotting out every detail of the next five years down to the minute. It is about knowing the bigger reason why you are starting your own business, why you've decided to do it now, who you are serving with your product and service, and what you are here to accomplish. It is getting positively and utterly clear on your mission. Once you're clear on that, the other pieces will more easily fall into place and you won't feel like you're constantly pushing a gigantic boulder up a mountain all on your own.

Surprisingly, getting clear is much easier than you think.

In his book, *Start with Why*, Simon Sinek explains how innovative and influential leaders and companies think completely differently from everyone else. In fact, they think completely the opposite of what's typical. They all start with *why*.

Sinek believes, "Very few people or companies can clearly articulate WHY they do WHAT they do. When I say WHY I don't mean to make money – that's a result. By WHY I mean what is your purpose, cause or belief? WHY does your company exist? WHY do you get out of bed every morning? And WHY should anyone care."

Sinek has found that the most innovative companies (Apple and Southwest Airlines) and influential leaders (Martin Luther King, Jr. and John F. Kennedy) had a very clear *why*, and that is what drove the *what* they did and *how* they did it. The what and how are secondary to the why however, most companies focus on what they do or make and how they do it and then wonder why they are not as successful.

When interviewing the women for this book, there was no doubt that their why was at the forefront of their minds. It is a constant driver and, in fact, it was their greatest motivational force during challenging times. This clarity also helped them define what success looked like for them, both professionally and personally.

If gaining clarity is so easy, you might ask, then why am *I* not clear yet?

I believe there is one major player when it comes to clarity and that is resistance created by the ego.

Resistance loves to make a grand and distracting entrance when you're in the midst of getting clear. When you're getting clear about the direction of your work and life, you inevitably will be doing things that push you outside your comfort zone. Your comfort zone is that place where everything is predicable, relatively certain and easy. This zone also doesn't provide much in the way of growth. Even if you're miserable with your job or relationship, when change is on the horizon, your ego jumps up and says, "But darling, what you have is fine. You're fine."

When the word *fine* enters your vocabulary – look out. Fine is such an emotionless reaction to being asked, "How are you?" Quite frankly, what is fine, anyway? It isn't *good*, it surely isn't *great*, but it is neither *bad* nor *crappy*, either. Fine is the response one gives you while also flashing that plastic smile resembling someone who's heavily sedated. Trust me, you don't want to go through life one more day just being fine.

However, once you start becoming clear, you will be compelled to move in the direction that inspires and, frankly, scares you. You will journey down a different path than the one you're currently weaving down. You might need to quit your job, quit your relationship, move cities, drop friends, sell off your belongings, learn skills that frighten you, speak on stages, speak to strangers, change your look, gain confidence, change your routine, give up caffeine, say yes, say no, learn a language, get a passport, or hire a therapist. Whatever it might be, the ego doesn't like change so it viciously fights to keep you where you are with muddled, foggy thinking. It keeps you confused so it can continue to run the show.

Clarity doesn't need to come all at once, although it's great when it does. However, the bigger picture may slowly become clear overtime as the fog drifts away and the full landscape of your dreams emerge. Remember, though, you don't need to have complete clarity to begin: the first glimpse of it is enough to begin the journey – so start.

Clarity in your why comes from knowing what ignites you, how you derive meaning from life, what makes you happy, how you define success and what motivates you. To paraphrase the philosopher Friedrich Nietzsche, she who has a strong enough why can figure out any how.

Challenge: Your Big Why

It's time to reflect on your big why. You may think you know what it is but it's worth digging a bit more to see if there is anything down deep that is really driving and motiving you. You can write it down or talk it out with a trusted friend.

1.   What is your why?
2.   Why do you want to start your own business?
3.   Why now?

You will need to drill down and continue to ask why several times to get to the root.

For instance, the conversation might look like this:

"What is my why?"

"My why is that I want to make $100,000 each year in my own business."

"Why?"

"So I can finally pay off my debt and buy a house?"

"Why?"

"So I can feel like I have more options."

"Really? Why does that matter?"

"Because I want to actually feel free and secure?"

"But why your own business? Isn't it easier to get a job?"

"Because I don't want to work for someone anymore?

"So..."

"Well I also see a need in the market."

"So what? Why you?"

"Because I know I have a lot to offer and I'm really excited about it."

"Why does this particular business idea speak to you though?"

"Because I really want to help people with ____."

"Why?"

"I know that by helping other people using my unique skills and talents, it'll make me happy and fulfilled and I will be contributing to the world in a bigger way."

As illustrated, it's important to drill down on your personal why. Why do you want to start a business and why this particular business right now.

Spotlight: Tami Dempsey On Discovering Her Why

For Pastor Tami her why came to her only after resigning from her position. A pastor's daughter and then a pastor's wife, Tami's life seemed to be heading in a predicable direction. She and her husband led a large ministry in Southern California, however her direction changed when she found a lump in her breast after having had breast cancer and one breast removed six years previously. She shared of that experience, "If I had only one year left to live, I wanted to spend it down in the trenches – getting my hands dirty – giving myself away to those that could not give in return." As a ministry leader you often deal more with politics and because of this elevated position, much is done for you. To her surprise, her husband felt similarly and they decided to resign from their positions as pastors of their church and move to Bulgaria to teach in the embassy school.

Within two weeks of teaching third grade, Tami discovered that several of the children were being abused. Sadly because she was in Bulgaria there was nothing they could legally do about it although everyone in the school was aware of the abuse. It broke her heart and she knew she had to do something. She decided to help the kids by teaching them about boundaries and the importance of valuing themselves. Every Monday she taught one particularly powerful lesson. She would bring in a crisp U.S. ten dollar bill and would ask them if anyone wanted the money. Everyone raised their hands. Then she would wrinkle it up and step on it and ask the question again. All hands would raise. Then she would roll the bill in mud, spit on it and damage it more and again ask the children if anyone wanted the bill. Of course, all hands raised to the sky. She kept asking them, "Why would you want a bill that has been so damaged?"

They would reply "because it's still a $10 bill". She used this example to explain that everyone was born with great value and no matter what happened in their life or what people did to them, their value is still great. She would follow it up by asking the kids to write the following affirmation at the top of all their papers, "I have great value". She changed these children's lives by her simple yet profound lessons.

When she came back to the United States she decided to take these lessons and create after school programs for abused kids. She is touching lives with her bigger why. As she shared through tears, "I'm motivated by the hurting children. I can do anything for the kids. If I make it about supporting myself, I freeze. They give me the courage and confidence to move through my fear and take the next bold, audacious step – the leap of faith that inevitably catapults me into living the next phase of my dream." Her why enables her to take significant leaps and bold action to not only build a business but to use her business to fulfill her bigger personal why.

Passion + Purpose + Meaning = Happiness

> "There is not one big cosmic meaning for all; there is only the meaning we each give to our life, an individual meaning, an individual plot, like an individual novel, a book for each person."
>
> —Anaïs Nin

One word came up more during my interviews than any other word. That word was *passion*. Even the women who were the toughest of nails spoke warmly about the love they have for what they do. The advice, "Follow your passion" and "You must have passion for what you do" was doled out like candy on Halloween night. Every person helped fill my bag with this sweet reminder.

Often our youth is where we can rediscover what lights our fire. If you look back —way back to when you were a child — there are glimmers of this passion. For author Jeryl Brunner, her passions were seen early on. She was a curious kid and always had a sense of wonder about the world. She would take the train from Westchester County into New York City to go the New York City Library which houses one of the largest collections outside the Library of Congress. She would pick a subject, select several books and lose herself in the topic. She derived incredible joy from these early adventures to the library. She has taken that curiosity and passion for learning and has created a successful career as a writer. In 2003, after nine years writing for *InStyle Magazine*, she decided to go out on her own and become a freelance travel writer and author. She has interviewed hundreds of some of the world's most fascinating people and has traveled all over the world. When she was just starting out on her own, she shared, "I just had to survive as a freelancer and I did what I had to do and took on loads of jobs." After a couple of years, she realized it wasn't about just surviving and decided to become selective in the projects that she would take and work only on the ones that she felt passionate about. She now focuses on projects that truly interest her. "It took a couple of years to grow comfortable in my freelancing skin but now I can finally confidently say this is something I can do," said Jeryl.

Jeryl's passion was evident from the very beginning and she has morphed her love of learning, researching, traveling and writing into her work and life.

As a kid, what did you do that you could be lost in for hours? What did you run home to tell your mom and dad about? What made you smile, laugh, jump up and down, scream, and get crazy-eyed focused about? What did you write in your diary? What dreams did you share with your BFF that you didn't want anyone else to know about? The seeds were planted way back then. You just need to tend, water and nourish that sweet little seedling to finally encourage it to fully bloom.

As you know, you don't need the perfect environment to allow it to bloom. You may have seen a gorgeous flower spring out of cement highway medium. Surroundings can look grey but when it's time to bloom, when it is ready to burst out, a flower will fully blossom.

Spotlight: Sheri Fink On Being Bullied to Blossoming

Sheri's path to her finding her passion came after an extremely bleak period in her life. She grew up in rural Virginia in a very poor family. Her entrepreneurial drive appeared early on when she would sell bracelets she made and write books. To Sheri, this felt normal, but her family didn't quite understand her. She was the first person in her family to go to college and she took it a step further and got her Master's degree as well. She landed what she calls a "sexy position," meaning she was proud of what she had accomplished and how well she was climbing the corporate ladder. However, she secretly hated it. She was raised to believe that "work is work" and everyone is unhappy with the jobs they were doing. You just sucked it up and did your job.

The secret she was also holding was that she was being bullied by another women in the company – a women she considered a friend. She couldn't believe what was happening to her. The woman went as far as slashing Sheri's tires. She tried everything to figure out how to deal with this difficult situation. She talked to her boss, spoke with human resources, and she read countless books. She wanted desperately to change this situation. One day she was driving to work and she burst into tears. All of her emotions and feelings surrounding this situation had caught up with her. While sobbing, she thought to herself, "I will do anything to change this experience with this woman."

In the midst of what she refers to as her "surrender moment," the story of a little rose came to her. In fact, it came pouring out of her. At a stop light, she started feverishly writing, grabbing every single piece of paper she could find in the car. She even resorted to using her body to transcribe her story by writing some of the prose on her leg. That day, however, was just the first step in Sheri's journey. She put the story away for over a year and kept saying, "After this or after that, then I'll do something with it." After participating in an inspiring seminar and reflecting on the question, "what will it take?" she decided to make her book a reality.

She published two books within a year and has been an Amazon.com #1 bestseller in her category. She has built an entire business around her books and doing what she loves, and her enthusiasm and passion is contagious. Sheri has spoken to over six thousand people and her story *The Little Rose Grows Up* has been turned into a screenplay. She has received countless letters from kids who thank her for her work and who share how it has changed their lives. As Sheri noted, "I was so in my head, so strategic and focused on what was best for others. I felt like a corporate robot and I wasn't being my authentic self. Now I get to amplify love and joy for children."

It may have taken a few years before she was clear on her next path, but once she was, her entire life turned around. She is living her definition of success. "Success for me is bouncing out of bed enthusiastic for life, creating experiences I love and that make me smile, creating deep meaningful connections, knowing I'm making a difference, and giving from the heart." She dreams of being the next Walt Disney. Why not?

Only you know what you're passionate about and you are the only one who will know when you find it. Jessica Herrin, founder of Stella and Dot, feels like she has finally found her perfect match. "Like love, you'll know if you've found 'the one'. It sounds lofty and grand but building a business takes so much commitment and effort. Only if you love it can you levitate yourselves over the obstacles that stand in the way of creating a business. You should do it because it is uniquely suited for you," Jessica shared in an interview for *Savor the Success* magazine.

Jenny Blake had what she called her "dream job" working at Google on Training and Career Development teams but she felt deep in her heart there was more for her. She never imagine becoming an entrepreneur however began exploring her passion for writing, sharing and coaching. Her love of books was evident from an early age when she would spend countless hours at the bookstore after school. A self-proclaimed book worm, she has always been on the lookout for just the right book "prescription" for whatever might be standing in her way and in the way of others. She knew that she wanted to write a book as well and it was time to take action. Being ever pragmatic, she decided to take a three-month sabbatical from Google to make her passion for writing and coaching work. She was incredibly busy those three months and thoughtfully considered her next steps. "I would forever regret not trying. I was willing to spend every last dime that I had to know that I had at least taken the leap, rather than just let my fears hold me back." She knew it was now or never and leapt. Although having lived her whole life in California she knew it was also the time to take on a new city and relocated to New York City, a dream she always held close. Jenny was drawn to passions that have been present her whole life and thoughtfully found a way to weave her love of writing and working with others into a business that she loves.

You will work hard, face challenges, and sometimes make sacrifices, so it's important you take a moment to reflect. Your business may become intimately entwined in your personal life, so decide if your idea and company is something you just like — or something you love.

Challenge: Tapping into Your Passion

Part 1: Rediscover What Ignites You

As a child, what did you love doing? For example: playing sports, dancing, painting, chatting with others, organizing your friends, reading, or composing music. List out everything that you can remember.

When you were in high school, what were your favorite courses? What were your favorite activities? Did you coach, mentor or volunteer? How did you spend your weekends? What did you daydream about? What did you want to do after high school? What did you want to study in college? What did you actually study in college? What were your favorite classes? What hobbies, sports, artistic endeavors, and social activities were you involved with that you loved?

What do you love doing now? What activities do you do that you can get lost in for hours? What do you daydream about? If you won the lottery tomorrow, what would you do with all that free time?

Part 2: Finding Passion through Daydreaming

Now, take out a piece of paper and write down everything you would love to do in life. It could be, "I would love to learn Italian" to "I would love to have fresh flowers in my home each week." Dream big: nothing is off-limits. Don't hold back and don't limit yourself because you don't know *how* you're going to accomplish it. Go for bold and outrageous. The bigger the better.

Once you have your completed list, post it some place where you can refer to it often. You may even want to share it with a close friend. Often, when we share and verbalize our dreams, we commit ourselves to them in a stronger way.

Our passions don't need to be relegated to our free time, childhood memories or our dreams. We can incorporate our passions into our work as well – once we clearly discover what they are.

Passion is the fuel and purpose is the vehicle that propels you forward. Purpose also acts as your internal GPS guiding you along your path. It is your big, personal *why*. Many people know what their purpose in life is from an early age, while others only discover it after years of varied experiences. Purpose is a deep knowing – a knowing that you are doing the work that you were meant to do. It's more than just a sense of satisfaction, it's deeper than that. Satisfaction is a great quality to have when it comes to work and keeps many people happily working in companies and for themselves for years. But purpose is a deep knowing that what you are doing transcends simply a position or reaching a particular goal. Of course, it is essential to set goals, but realize that the journey itself towards a goal provides significant meaning and happiness.

So you're now doing something you're passionate about and, hopefully, are damn good at it. You add purpose to what you're doing and *voila!* You have meaning.

The meaning of life *is* the quintessential philosophical question. Meaning involves discovering why you're here, using your unique talents in such a way that is worthwhile to your life and, potentially, others' lives as well, and actively fulfilling the purpose you feel is calling you. Meaning is powerful motivation in your life. Meaning gets you out of bed when you're otherwise wiped out. It keeps you going when all signs tell you to turn around and go home. It is what connects us to our humanity and gives us a sense of fulfillment that otherwise cannot be filled by material possessions. Meaning is purpose elevated. When you've cleared the path to meaningful work, watch out, because the magic has officially begun.

Whenever you're engaged in meaningful activities, there is one potent benefit. And that benefit is happiness. Tal Ben-Shahar, former professor at Harvard University where his classes on Positive Psychology and The Psychology of Leadership were among the most popular courses in the University's history, is a leader in the field of positive psychology. He describes happiness in his book *Happier* as the "overall experience of pleasure and meaning." Meaning provides long-term happiness and is derived from engaging in something that has great intrinsic value to you.

Further research in the field of positive psychology has shown a significant link between doing meaningful work and increased levels of happiness. As we know by the proliferation of books and documentaries on happiness, it isn't just something that is a nice-to-have; it is essential for good health as well. Research has shown time and again that happiness improves physical health and promotes resilience and stamina —three things every entrepreneur needs. Studies show that happier workers have lower levels of the stress hormone, cortisol, that nasty chemical that wreaks havoc within our systems when it's constantly secreted during times of stress. Cortisol is responsible for causing or exacerbating numerous modern world ailments such as cardiovascular disease, diabetes and cancer.

Doing something that has great intrinsic value to you is highly individual and you need to discover on your own through serious reflection, thoughtful journaling and perhaps meditation what gives your life meaning, what lights your internal fire, and what makes you happy. Only you know what brings meaning to your life.

So what makes you happy? Can you easily answer that question? If not, it's time to do some exploring and excavating.

When you find that purposeful and meaningful work that lights you up, you open yourself to a life full of success, abundance and happiness.

Defining Success

> "I believe you are your work. Don't trade the stuff of your life, time, for nothing more than dollars. That's a rotten bargain."
>
> —Rita Mae Brown

The traditional trifecta of success for many men is money, status and power. You only have to watch one episode of MTV Cribs to have this point grossly reinforced. The tides are slowly and quietly shifting, though, and even more enlightened men of our time define success differently. For women, however, success means something quite different. Research has shown that finding meaning in the work we do is of utmost importance for women. That's how we define success.

I asked each of the women how they defined personal and professional success. Not one woman spoke of power or fame. Only a few spoke about money, but only as way of gauging the progress of their business and not as something that solely drives them. Each woman had a very personal definition of success.

Megan Burns, Founder of Operations Strategy Consulting and the Naptime CEO, shared, "There are revenue and growth goals, of course, but what makes me feel successful is knowing that, without a doubt, I'm living out my purpose. Success by the world's standards or not, I'm on this Earth for a purpose, and I'm doing it."

For Lynn Perkins, founder of UrbanSitter, success involves both solving a problem and working with people she likes. Lynn is proud of the company she has built. Success means "building a team I like to work with because it's all about the people," she shared.

Jennifer Ferguson of Symphony Financial, who has started three separate businesses in the insurance field, defines success differently than others in her field who view the insurance business as strictly transactional. "Success to me is knowing I am making a difference in the lives of the people I meet every day, regardless of whether or not we work together," Jennifer shared. Growing up, as she puts it, "very poor," she always knew that she wanted to create a business where she could help and educate families so that they didn't have the financial struggles she was straddled with at a young age, and to help people avoid the stress and strain that comes from financial concerns.

For some women like Yoga Code founder Jackie Dumaine, it is all about the tribe. Jackie views success as following through with her vision, with her dream, and creating change in the world. "It's all about creating a connected team of people who believe in your vision and creating a community of people who are inspired by what you do. This in turn inspires them to create something unique themselves," she shared. "It's all about creating cool teams and a cool tribe."

For Diana Rothschild of NextKids, a co-working space with childcare, she originally thought success was all about profit margins. Her business school training instilled the financial aspect as one of the main metrics of quantifying success. Diana has come to realize that success is much more than numbers on a spreadsheet – it's about having a significant impact on a wide range of societal issues, living her values and being home for dinner with her family. "Success was centered around making money. Now it's about changing the world in a positive way, having fun doing it, and making money – in that order," Diana shared.

Your definition of success can change and evolve over time as well. For Carly Blalock of Carly & Co, an interior design company success for her is constantly evolving as she reinvents her business and herself. She calibrates after every project whether it was successful. As she shared, "You can never stop changing. There are opportunities everyday to learn and put yourself in new subject areas to learn even more." Success for Carly involves change and growth and she's been able to explore this through expanding her business into retail and furniture design.

So now it's your turn. How do you define success? In order to discover your personal definition, it's time to do some internal excavation.

Challenge: How Do You Define Success?

What does success look like for you? You may already be there. You may have a picture of it in your mind or beautifully composed on a vision board. It may be a moving target, ever changing and unfolding. Take a moment and reflect on what success means to you and what it looks like.

Defining success personally:
Do you have an active social life?
Are you spending a lot of time with your family?
Are you physically active?
Are you content?
Are you energized?
How do you feel?
Are you living in a particular location, type of house, or freewheeling it out of a suitcase?
Are you volunteering and taking time to give back?
Do you make time for yourself?
Are you going on regular vacations?

Defining success professionally
Are you doing what you love?
Are you working independently, or do you have a team?
Who are you serving?
If you have a team, are they functioning well and thriving?
Who are your clients and customers?
How many people do you serve?
Is your product in several different markets?
Do you have a global reach?
Are you getting positive feedback?
Are you making a difference in your community and/or in the world?
How do you feel about your business and your clients/customers?
What are your financial milestones?

Any other developmental milestones?

Is there anything that you're willing to sacrifice to achieve success?

What will your life look like three, five, ten years from now?

In your mind or on a piece of paper, paint a very detailed picture of what your life will look like at each milestone? Use all your senses when imagining what it will look like. When you have clearly defined what success is in your life you will better navigate your life in that direction.

Finding Freedom

I asked each of the women I interviewed what their favorite part about being an entrepreneur was. Time and again, the answer was: freedom.

This freedom meant not being told what to do, but also included the freedom of expression and creativity and the freedom to come up with an idea and act on it immediately rather than having to ask for permission or dealing with bureaucratic red tape. They may be free from the typical nine-to-five fixed schedule, but that does not mean they're working less. They are often working twice as long and twice as hard – yet loving every minute of it.

For Cynthia Nerangis, being an entrepreneur makes perfect sense. "Where do I begin? There are so many things I love about being an entrepreneur. The ability to have the flexibility to manage my own schedule, to use my creativity, and to provide my expertise to clients are what I enjoy about being an entrepreneur." She especially enjoys the flexibility to travel and not having to request time off to do so. Cynthia, who is Greek American with family still in Greece, enjoys traveling and values the importance of taking time off to recharge. "Success is also stepping away from time to time," she shared. She founded LemonLime Consulting in 2004 which specializations in preparing companies and people to work internationally. She clearly is one who found the perfect blend of her passions for varied cultures, international travel, business and the freedom to do it all.

As Eleanor Roosevelt once said, "With freedom comes responsibility," and successful women entrepreneurs know that this full ownership also includes being fully responsible for when things don't go well. But they're willing to take the seemingly bad with the incredible good. You won't see them trading in their new-found freedom to return to a corporate gig. Many women actually quipped they are now "unemployable" – no one would ever hire them because they would now make terrible employees.

It is the unencumbered ability to take any creative idea and put it out in the world that attracted Alexandra Franzen to start her own business. "One of the best things about being my own boss is that if I get a brilliant idea, there's no impediment to doing it. No 'manager' who needs to sign off on the project. No hurdles in the way." She is easily someone you could lovingly call a free spirit, although she calls herself a writer, teacher, author and creative minx.

After college, Alexandra got her dream job in broadcasting. Fairly quickly she realized that the cubical life was too structured for her. It was the middle of the recession and she felt both sad and guilty about not being happy in such a plum position. Her colleagues were getting laid off and she felt like she should feel grateful for just having a job. At the end of 2009, her eyes were opened to a world she had never considered — a world where men and women were creating businesses and designing their own lives around their creativity. She was drawn to the notion of empowering others through writing and helping to create online brands. She realized she was meant to be doing this all along but just had not realized it until now. Her last day of a traditional job was April 1, 2010 — April Fool's Day. She doesn't see herself as simply a conventional writer, but as a communication specialist. As Alexandra puts it, "I want every word that I write – and every word that I speak – to leave the people around me in better condition than I found them. And I want to inspire others to communicate that way, too." She believes success is leaving this Earth in a better condition than when you arrived. As she poetically explained, "One of the simplest things you can do to make the world a better place is to write and speak with more clarity, purpose and compassion. It's not about perfection. Just perpetual refinement." Inspired by Mister Rogers and Ru Paul, Alexandra's writing is rich, poetic, heartfelt and most importantly fun. If you've had a chance to read her musings you know she is definitely delivering on her promise of leaving the world in a better, more beautiful, place. And, for anyone who wants to use language to add color and meaning to their own life and create a thriving profession in the process, she is model for making that happen.

Spotlight: Kassie Rempel On How Shoes Make a Woman

Ever since she was a little girl, Kassie Rempel has loved shoes. Although she spent many years in accounting — a notoriously conservative profession — she found that shoes and accessories could help her express more of her personality. Ultimately she knew she wanted to figure out her passion and make that her profession, however, she wasn't comfortable putting money behind her idea just yet.

Luckily, she was given an opportunity to help build a business for someone she knew who was opening an exercise studio and spa. Helping build a business on someone else's dime gave her the experience, skills and self-confidence to start her own company. Kassie knew she wanted to build a company around her first love: shoes. In 2003, she boldly wrote a letter to the owner of her favorite catalog, *Wisteria*, saying, "I love your product. Would you have any advice for someone going into the catalogue business industry?" she recalls. Although she had no introduction to the owner, he wrote a three-page letter back giving her everything she needed to start. He shared with her books to read and how to determine expenses, and gave her the names and contact information for his printers, list brokers and others. He even told her that he had already made calls to them and that they were expecting her call. "The three page letter became my blueprint," Kassie shared. And that is how Simply Soles, an e-commerce shoe boutique, was created.

After all these years, her love of shoes has not waned. She went from shoe buyer (selling Simply Soles in 2012) to full-time shoe designer, launching lillybee in 2008. In typical entrepreneurial fashion, Kassie has started another business she's excited about as well. She recently launched Kassie's Closet, a styling and shopping site, as a vehicle to share her skills and knowledge to help others. "I want to help women look and feel good so they have the confidence to pursue their passion and purpose," she said. It's more than simply fashion for Kassie; she wants to give back by empowering women through personal style and fashion so they can feel they can do and be anything they want to be.

Motivation Beyond Self

Even though you may be starting a business to fulfill a personal aspiration or to create freedom in your life, there is often another layer to the story.

From a simple question, "What motivates you?" came some of the most thoughtful and inspiring answers. What I heard was that what kept women in the game was something larger than themselves. What motivated them was the ability to impact the lives of others, to support their families and communities, and to be able to give back in meaningful ways.

For entrepreneurs in the fitness industry, it is often easier to witness the impact they have on their clients and customers. Erika Bloom, founder of the popular New York City Pilates studio Erika Bloom Studio, shared that she is not only motivated by her own personal desires, but, as she put it, "in seeing the change in clients, in their bodies, and how they feel. It's rewarding and highly motivating."

Similarly, Jill Dailey McIntosh, founder of the Dailey Method, is motivated by the people she serves. The Dailey Method is a ballet barre exercise class she launched in San Francisco in 2000 which has grown significantly through the years with locations now expanding beyond the West Coast. As Jill shared, "I'm motivated always to learn more about the human body, to evolve the method through continuing education. I'm motivated to provide the absolute best method for the body." Jill isn't only interested in helping her clients achieve physical results; she is passionate about building confidence in the women who have made dramatic changes in not just their bodies, but in their lives. In 2009, she wanted to further empower women who wanted to start a business through her franchising program. "Success is not built on monetary gain or being well-known, I went into this thinking I'd have one studio. Success is helping empower women in so many ways, giving women the chance to have successful businesses and creating community."

Tina Calloway, founder of Urban FarmGirls Design Co., a garden design company, was initially motivated to start and succeed in business out of necessity. In early 2008, Tina's world was about to crumble. She was a successful artist with a studio in San Francisco whose work was shown in popular galleries across the city. Within a matter of a few months, she lost her studio space due to the recession's impact on commercial real estate, was laid off from her part-time job teaching art to adults with disabilities, and her husband – her high school sweetheart – walked out. She was devastated but had to keep it together because she had a young daughter to look after. She turned to gardening for solace. Without the space to create her art and no part-time income to speak of, she started doing landscape design work and gardening for friends. People were so impressed by her unique blend of art and gardening that she quickly started getting paid jobs. She also created handmade pots made of recycled materials and filled them with local plants that caught the eye of Whole Foods and other local vendors.

Now, five years later she runs her business out of a massive space in San Francisco, has a team of loyal designers and assistants, and is in high-demand. She and her teenage daughter are thriving. As Tina casually sat down with me in her studio with her dog on her lap, a sense of peace filled her entire warehouse space. She reflected, "Success is fulfilling, happy work. For me it is about doing work that is meaningful, that benefits the community I live in, purposeful, creative and that creates a living for myself, my daughter and provides jobs for others." No one knows what the future holds for Tina, but that doesn't phase her. "There is a certain amount of unknown when it comes to business, the artist in me likes the unknown part. You have to have courage to always move forward and be open to change in business." Although Tina embraces the unknown, she is clear that doing meaningful work while supporting her family and contributing to the community is of utmost importance.

Spotlight: Meg Gill On Passion and Her New Role

Meg Gill is no typical Ivy League startup founder. Although she holds a degree from Yale University, she has humble beginnings — and an even humbler love for beer. As co-founder of Golden Road Brewing in Los Angeles, Meg is the youngest female brewery owner in the world. Spotting a void in the brewing industry in the LA area, Meg moved from the craft-brewery-rich Northern California to start her company. "I did it because it felt natural and I felt so passionate about it." Meg further shared, "I didn't even know I was taking risks. I didn't realize I was blindly challenging the norm and myself."

Her passion superseded the fact that the beer industry is dominated by men, which includes the more blue-collar distributors network. Fortunately, growing up from humble beginnings in Virginia, she is able to speak the same language of the distributors with whom she has developed great relationships.

Her passion has expanded from beer to the the water that produces it. An accomplished swimmer and avid surfer, Meg found herself one day out on the water after a storm. Not realizing that that is a surfing "no no," she ended up witnessing first hand the trash that washes up from storm drains. Surrounded by trash, bottles, and more, her mind was blown. That experience changed her, and she decided to team up with the environmental group, Heal the Bay, to raise not only awareness, but funds for something she loves.

She has been surprised how others have reached out to her to speak on her status as a pioneering woman in a male-dominated field. She has taken this new role – as role model– with the same humility as she has with other areas of life. Humble yet knowing the importance of her new role, she is happy to bring awareness to the lack of female leaders not only in her field, but in business ownership in general.

Spotlight: Whitney Johnson
On Daring to Dream

Whitney Johnson has truly traveled far from her Northern Californian roots. Two year after graduating from Brigham Young University, she and her husband were off to New York City so he could study molecular biology at Columbia University. Because his PhD program would take over five years to complete and they were living on a pithy stipend, Whitney knew she needed to find a job. She didn't want just any job though, she decided she wanted an office job in financial services. She was in the center of the financial world (when in Rome, right?) however had no business experience. At that time, she was a twenty-seven year old woman with a music degree and found her only option was to become a secretary. She ended up landing a sales assistant role at Smith Barney working alongside Ivy Leaguers who were mostly men. Even with all their fancy degrees and accolades, Whitney knew they were no smarter than she was and decided then and there that she could dream bigger. As she wrote in her book *Dare, Dream, Do*: "I may not have a degree from Princeton, and I may not be an engineer, but I can be successful on Wall Street". Her tenacity and desire to dream and play big paid off and by the time she was in her 40s she had risen to become a double-ranked Institutional Investor sell-side analyst, a frequent contributor to the Harvard Business Review and finally a co-founder, along with the renowned management thinker Clayton M. Christensen, of Rose Park (Disruptive Innovation Fund).

Whitney didn't stop with going after her own dreams. In 2006 she launched a blog titled Dare To Dream where she encourages and dares women to dream and take action on those dreams. She followed it up with the book, *Dare, Dream, Do* that contains the stories collected from the blog and guidance for women to follow their own ambitious dreams – whatever they may be.

Whitney further gives back through investing in startups and her charitable work. Incredibly gracious, Whitney shared her views on why there is a dearth of female role models for entrepreneurs, "We often have an impulse to help people in the exotic faraway, while neglecting the woman living across the street." She also believes that we'd be much better off if we look at role models in a "modular fashion" meaning we look to different women for different needs. She believes that men are a bit better at looking towards other in a modular way rather than trying to glean everything from a single individual. Don't forget there may be an entire generation of women you may be neglecting. "There are young people that would have intimidated me when I was in my 20s. Now, rather than being abashed, I just think how privileged I am to know and work with them." Whitney is a model of venturing a path without the typical skill set required, doing her own thing authentically and with style and helping others dare to discover what they truly want out of their lives.

Gaining clarity may not happen for you in one day, or even this year. It can be a process that takes thoughtful reflection and time. You need to ponder what you love doing, what activities and projects might you derive meaning from, what motivates you, and how you define success. You need to truly ask yourself and answer honestly: "How do I want to feel?". Often the core feelings that you want to hold in your heart day in and day out can provide revealing answers to you. They can clear the fog of confusion and overwhelm and lead you to the path where you most want to be.

I realize that these are heavy questions, but it is vital that you begin to work on clearing the path, hacking away the overgrown brush, so that you can start the journey. By answering the questions posed in this chapter, you will be one step closer towards your goals and dreams.

Inspiration Library

Music
Freedom by George Michael
Brighter Than the Sun by Colbie Callout
Can't Hold Us by Macklemore (feat Ryan Lewis)
If I Had a $1,000,000 by Barenaked Ladies

Movies
I Am
The Way

Books
How Remarkable Women Lead by Joanna Barsh and Susie
   Cranston
Happier: Can You Learn to be Happy? by Tal Ben-Shahar
*Happiness Project: Or, Why I Spent a Year Trying to Sing in the
   Morning, Clean My Closets, Fight Right, Read Aristotle, and
   Generally Have More Fun* by Gretchen Rubin
*The Gifts of Imperfection: Let Go of Who You Think You're
   Supposed to Be and Embrace Who You Are* by Brené Brown
*Dare, Dream, Do: Remarkable Things Happen When You Dare
   to Dream* by Whitney Johnson
The Desire Map: A Guide to Creating Goals with Soul by
   Danielle Laporte

CHAPTER 5

Get Going (Behavior)

"Twenty years from now you will be more
disappointed by the things that you didn't do than
by the ones you did do, so throw off the bowlines,
sail away from safe harbor, catch the trade winds
in your sails. Explore, dream, discover."
                                —Attributed to Mark Twain

Congratulations! You've gotten your mindset on board with
your dreams and have clarified why you're even remotely
interested in going out on your own. Now you're ready to begin
taking some action. You can think, dream and visualize all day
long, but until you act on your dreams, you won't see them come
alive in the world. They will simply be left behind as interesting
ideas you once had. I want more for you.

If in the previous chapter you found that clarity didn't appear to
you in a dream, come in a flash of brilliance, or materialize as you
mindlessly doodled on a napkin, take heart. Clarity can be tough
but don't let the lack of it currently stop you. Remember these wise
words from the author Marcus Buckingham: "If you want to be
clear, act." Begin exploring your why and passions by taking steps
forward immediately. In doing so, often clarity will appear.

With all entrepreneurs, both women and men, there are
particular behaviors that take them from the dreamer to the

doer. These behaviors include: the willingness to embrace risk, constant forward-moving action, discovering and working in one's flow, and creating discipline.

Welcome Risk

> "The fishermen know that the sea is dangerous and the storm terrible, but they have never found these dangers sufficient reason for remaining ashore."
> — Vincent van Gogh

Let's get something clear: When we're discussing risk, I'm not talking about jumping out of a plane or wandering into a dark ally in an unsavory neighborhood at 4 a.m. Although, at times, you may have the same visceral reaction to aspects of your business. You may feel anxiety, fear, panic or even sheer terror. The risk I'm talking about is a level of risk tolerance that all entrepreneurs adopt. You cannot run away from it. It is your ticket to enter this crazy circus. Without taking some risk, you are relegated to standing outside while everyone else is inside enjoying the show.

But don't worry: you don't need to take massive leaps to gain admittance – at least, not yet. There is a spectrum of risk. The level which you might be comfortable at may differ from your entrepreneurial friends. You may be comfortable with quitting your job with only an idea in hand and a deep knowingness that you'll make it work. Or, you may begin by finding an investor or partner to launch your business. Or, you may take all of your savings and pour it into the development of a product without capital from anyone else. Or, you may keep your day job and slowly launch a business on the side. Each of these scenarios involves risk. You just need to decide where you're comfortable at on this spectrum.

You may also be more risk-loving than you think. Don't underestimate yourself. Simply taking an idea and giving it the consideration to make it into something is a huge start. The fact that you are following your passion can be seen as risky from the outside. Lovingly pat yourself on the back for even considering it in the first place. Outside of our blossoming businesses, we take risks all the time — whether we realize it or not. Deciding on a major in college is risky. Changing jobs is risky. Dating and then deciding on a partner is risky. Buying a house is risky. Having kids is risky. Going to Whole Foods on a Sunday afternoon is risky. Traveling is risky. Hosting a dinner party for your foodie friends is risky. Driving a car is risky. Not carrying an umbrella in Portland is risky. We take risks all the time, whether we realize it or not.

Lynn Perkins, mom of twin boys and founder of UrbanSitter, candidly admitted that she is fairly risk adverse in her personal life but takes much bolder risks in her professional life. It's a good thing she knows that about herself. She has definitely taken risks professionally, moving to unfamiliar cities to take roles in fledgling startups, leaving the startup world to get experience in a large corporate settings, and eventually founding two startups of her own. UrbanSitter, a site that links parents with local babysitters, is Lynn's second company. She founded the company based on something she and her friends were struggling with: locating a trusted sitter or nanny. She found that she and her friends could easily make restaurant reservations online in a instant but would spend days trying to secure a babysitter to watch the kids. She saw a need and worked to see if it was viable through speaking with technologists and people who market to moms, as well as directly to moms and sitters themselves. She buffered some of the risk by doing adequate market research and teaming up with quality people. Although some people would shy away from attaining venture funding, she knew if she wanted to grow the business she needed to secure funding. Once her beta site proved to be a hit, she was able to attract investors and she was off.

Sharon Schneider, founder of Moxi Jean, an upscale online consignment store for children's clothes, notes that you can't underestimate how scary and difficult launching a business can be. Although she was scared, she summoned up the courage to make the leap with three kids at home. "I was a 35 year old mom with three kids. There is no option of sleeping on the couch in an office and eating Ramen noodles," said Sharon. Unlike entrepreneurs without such responsibilities at home, she had to figure out how she could make her company and her home life work. She shared that she had to evaluate the risk and then finally said, "Screw it." She has an "irrational belief in herself," as she puts it — something all entrepreneurs must possess if they are going to be successful.

For Mauria Finley of Citrus Lane, a subscription service for parents that delivers baby and children's products directly to their door, she knew it was the right time to take a big risk. "Deciding to take the plunge was a challenge. I had a really great job, a great team, and was comfortable," she shared. After fifteen years in companies such as Netscape, AOL, Paypal, and eBay, among others, she knew she had to take a leap of faith and leave the comforts of a job. She teamed up with another female technology veteran and was able to raise the seed capital to launch Citrus Lane. Mauria could have easily stayed within the cozy confines of working within a company, but she felt compelled to venture out on her own in a big way.

Ambition and beef are two words that come to mind when I think of Anya Fernald. She is the force behind BelCampo which is on a mission to produce sustainable food on an unprecedented scale. She has a sustainable meat company headquartered in Northern California that includes a series of butcher shops, a ranch in Uruguay, and an eco-lodge in Belize where she also produces chocolate, coffee and rum. She runs a massive organization with the ambitious goal of serving as a financial case study to prove that sustainable food can be a profitable business. The famous chef Alice Waters has called Anya "fearless" and someone with a "real pioneer mentality."

Anya loves challenges — the bigger the better. "I like to take risks. I enjoy proving people wrong," Anya said confidently. Today, thanks to her risk-taking and bold nature, Anya is making an impact on both the sustainable food industry and the Slow Food movement.

Spotlight: Sue Chen On Swimming with Sharks

Taking risks doesn't scare Sue Chen, founder and CEO of Nova Medical Products. In fact, she goes after it. In 1993, when she was only twenty-three years old, Sue founded a medical equipment company that provides stylish designs for people using mobility equipment. At that time, "the industry was dominated by white males typically in their 50s" she recalled. She found it challenging to be taken seriously by her peers in an industry that had seen very little change over the years. But she was driven to build her company and to help her customers. Today, she has grown her company to sixty employees and has become an industry leader in Mobility and Bathroom Safety products. "You have to be a little bit crazy," Sue shared about starting a company. She is pushing her mission of helping people who become immobile and changing the landscape of industry through technology and innovation, something you don't often hear in this industry. She believes that men aren't the only ones who can be risk takers and adventurers and she definitely has proven that women can be just as daring — professionally and personally. Besides climbing Mount Kilimanjaro, Sue has taken up diving with sharks and has become an outspoken advocate for shark conservation as the Director of Shark Savers.

Risk and fear go hand and hand. Fear creeps in when we put ourselves in risky situations. But don't forget: fear should be saved for times when you're being chased by a mountain lion, driving too fast on a wet highway, or when you enter Macy's on Christmas Eve (okay, perhaps not the latter for anyone other than me). Fear is a signal for keeping us safe in *perceived* risky situations. Is following your passion the same as being followed by a stranger? Is jumping into starting a business the equivalent of base jumping? You need to ask yourself: *What am I so afraid of?*

Successful female entrepreneurs know the importance of making calculated and thoughtful risks regardless if doing so scares them. Often, they know that the fear associated with it is a sign of excitement at overcoming the next challenge or the novelty of trying something totally new.

Now it's your turn. It's time to step outside your comfort zone and embrace more risk. It may only be to place a toe outside you're cozy circle, but that is a great place to start.

Challenge: Let's Get Down to Some Risky Business

Determine where you are at on the risk-o-meter. What do you consider risky but are willing to try anyway, and what do you consider to be too risky to even consider?

A little heart racing is a good thing as it means you're stepping outside your comfort zone. But if you take a trip to the ER with chest pains, perhaps you've gone a bit too far outside what's healthy for you right now.

Exercise your risk muscle:

Risk is a muscle that you can strengthen through exercise and practice. Where can you flex a bit of your risk-taking muscle? What activities can you take on that stretches you a bit further?

Let's have some fun.

1. This week, I want you to do one thing that pushes you outside your comfort zone. It may be sitting in a cafe alone with no phone, computer or book for a half hour. Perhaps you go to a networking event and introduce yourself to no less than ten strangers. Maybe you call someone you admire and ask them a few questions about business, their leadership style or how they've integrated family and work. You may want to chat to your local bank about loan options. Or, perhaps you even go test drive a car you've been secretly eyeing. Whatever you decide, make sure to put it on the calendar and do it.

2. After a month of weekly risk challenges, begin to do one thing each day that is new or outside your comfort zone. Continue with similar items from above but also include some novel items. Novelty keeps you on your toes and will also prevent you from getting in a creative rut. You can visit a new coffee shop, buy a different brand of soap, look at different industries for marketing ideas, listen to a different genre of music, call a person you've admired (professionally or personally) from afar, try a different yoga studio, call a customer for feedback, wear a colorful scarf, or dress up to go to the grocery store.

You will find that through taking small risks regularly and doing things that are uncomfortable and novel, you will radically increase your self-confidence and boost your creativity as well.

Take Action

> "A ship is always safe at the shore – but that is
> NOT what it is built for."
> —Albert Einstein

Where many great ideas die is in the execution. Taking action on your idea is not optional – it's absolutely crucial. Otherwise, it simply stays a nice idea. Action is something you have to do daily. In his book *Getting Things Done*, David Allen shares, "You can't do a project. You can only do the next step." What often happens with the most well-intentioned entrepreneur is that she gets overwhelmed by the complexity and sheer amount of work that is required in starting and maintaining a business. Your to-do list might be several pages long, but you need to keep moving forward. You have to keep at it, little by little, a step every day.

In her book, *Wealthy Spirit*, Chellie Campbell talks about the importance of taking action. She uses the clever metaphor of sending out ships as a way to achieve your goals. As she describes it, in ninetieth-century London, merchants would build ships to send off to visit foreign ports to trade and purchase spices, silk, gold and more. They never sent just one ship because there was always a chance that the ship wouldn't make it back. Once the ships were sent off they had no way to communicate with them until they arrived safely back at port, hopefully loaded with treasure. The merchants' fortunes were made upon their safe return. This is where the expression, "I'm waiting for my ship to come in," comes from.

Some people head down to the docks expecting their ship to come in full of bountiful, beautiful treasure only to discover they never sent any ships out. How do you expect to receive anything if you just stand by the water wishing for a boat full of gold to arrive at the dock? In order to make your fortune, you need to send out ships. Not just one ship but several ships, and not just on one day, but everyday. Campbell believes that by developing a habit of sending out ships daily, knowing that some may not come back but hopeful others will return, you will be ever closer to your goals. As she writes, "I prefer the image of breaking the champagne bottle and waving goodbye to a proud clipper ship on a beautiful spring day as it sets forth on my behalf. And then celebrating the ship's safe arrival with all my wealth."

For you, sending out ships may mean making sales calls or sending emails for feedback on your product or service. You may send out ships that look like making coffee dates with people of influence. Whatever your ships may be, make it a point to send them out thoughtfully and frequently.

You may not always be confident or even clear in the actions you are taking, but often you just need to dive in. The more ships you send out to sea, the more likely one or more will deliver something grand.

Another way to propel yourself into action, especially on those days where you'd prefer to just sit in front of the TV mindlessly flipping through channels, is the Fifteen-Minute Rule. Tell yourself that you just have to do something for fifteen minutes – say work on a blog post, make sales calls, input your expenses – and after the time is up you can determine whether or not you want keep going. Those first fifteen minutes may be all you need to push through a project or get you into a flow to get it done. Fifteen minutes isn't a huge commitment but often just enough to get you into a project or task you've been avoiding. It is so often the start that stops most people so just get started.

Whatever system or metaphor that spurs you into action, find one that speaks to you. When Suzi Pomerantz, executive coach and author, started out twenty years ago, she faced her share of challenges. She was a 24 year-old leadership coach and her clients were mostly men over fifty at the peak of their careers. She was keenly aware of the looks her clients would give as they stared at her with crossed arms. "Who is this little girl and what does she have to teach me?" Suzi shared on what they must have been thinking. She was able to stand her ground and blew their socks off with what she could teach them. She says her naivety was a blessing because "I didn't know what I didn't know. Knowing what I know now, I might have been too scared to start," said Suzi. She had a company and clients before she even realized she was starting a business. When starting a business you often have to "act first and think later," shared Suzi.

Carly Blalock, interior designer, when sharing her views on success stated, "Successful entrepreneurs make a decision in six seconds, then they're done. They will take action right away. Where women tend to over think it and talk themselves out of it in the process." She also cautions that women sometimes let their emotional attachment to their business "take them sideways" rather than thinking in a more black and white, detached manner.

When speaking about action, I want you to also begin acting like an entrepreneur, as though you're already at that point where you envision yourself a few years down the road. Simply stated, you become an entrepreneur by mindfully acting like one today. If you've ever seen the movie *Boiler Room*, the concept of "act as if" is weaved throughout the first half of the movie when the main character, Seth Davis, played by Giovanni Ribisi starts out as a broker at a financial services firm. Without any financial services experience to speak of, Davis is thrown into a broker position cold-calling people on the phone who are twice his age. His mentors coach him into "acting as if" he already is a top producer, driving fancy cars and living the opulent life. Granted, the movie is a dark tale about corruption and greed, but the concept of "act as if" is one that will surely stick with you after watching it.

Challenge: Get Going

"The journey of a thousand miles begins with a single step."
— Lao Tzu

Often we just need a small nudge to move us into action through that first step.

Get out a sheet of paper. No really... stop and find a piece of blank paper and a pen.

What action or actions can you take today to move your business forward?

Answer the following questions:

1. **What will I do today?** Make is as specific as possible and use action verbs. (Don't use weak, disempowering words like "try" "think" or "ponder.")

2. **By when?** Be specific, set a date and put it on your calendar.

3. **What is the very first step?** That first step sets things in motion. It may be as simple as "Open up Google and type..."

And don't forget: it's not only about the first step; it is about constantly taking that first step and then subsequent steps on your journey. Step by step, and you'll be briskly moving forward in no time.

Exercise inspired by *Do More Great Work: Stop the Busywork: Start The Work That Matters* by Michael Bungay Stainer

Get Into the Flow

Being in the flow is a magical thing. You instantly know when you're in this state. Your work is effortless. You feel fully engaged and alive. You get lost in your work as time passes unnoticed. It may even feel and appear to others like you're on drugs or in some altered state. That is flow.

In his legendary and frequently referenced work, Mihaly Csikszentmihalyi, observed that people can achieve an altered state when they are "in a groove" or "in the zone." Anyone can achieve this state, including writers, athletes, musicians, artists, rock climbers or even factory workers. But what exactly is this altered state, and how can you create it?

To create this optimal experience, you first have to put your energy and attention on a goal. When you invest this time on the goal and use your well-matched skills to work towards it, you are setting yourself up to get into a flow state. Next, it's the pursuit of the goal and the period of concentration, struggle and overcoming of challenges which is what "people find to be the most enjoyable times of their lives," Csikszentmihalyi posits.

If you could identify what promotes a flow-like state, one where you are immersed in an enjoyable task while moving your business forward, wouldn't you regularly seek out these conditions? Well, thankfully, Csikszentmihalyi has identified five conditions for us. They are:

1. Clear, attainable yet stretch goals
2. Intrinsic motivation built into the task
3. Ability to concentrate on a particular topic
4. Ability to challenge you and your skills
5. Immediate feedback

An entrepreneurial friend of mine, Karen Hancock of KMH Makes, is a jewelry designer and lifestyle entrepreneur. She finds her flow state frequently when she enters her studio. Your flow activities may not produce creative pieces like Karen's work, but there are likely flow- inducing projects that put you in a similar state. Let's use Karen as an example and walk through the five conditions. You will inevitability see parallels in your own work.

As Csikszentmihalyi notes, it's difficult to enter into flow without clear goals. It's important that these goals are attainable but still a bit of a stretch. If the goals are too far out of reach, however, it may be discouraging, frustrating and difficult to find your flow. Conversely, easily met goals may make you feel good momentarily (quick wins), but you won't enter that beautiful state of flow. For Karen, when she steps into her studio, she usually has a particular piece in mind that she wants to work on. Her goal for a particular day may be to complete one aspect of a piece in an allotted time period.

To induce flow, there must be an intrinsic motivation built into the task at hand to create flow. Something other than checking it off your to-do list must motivate you. For Karen, just finishing a piece has internal motivation because it elicits pride in completion and the creative joy of designing and making something beautiful to share with others.

In order to find yourself in a state of flow, it is crucial to have the space to concentrate on a particular topic or task. If you're working in a chaotic or disruptive environment, it is much more difficult to get into your groove. Karen finds Stephen King's advice on the importance of having space to work and dream and she particularly loves his one surprising requirement. As Stephen King muses in his book, *On Writing: A Memoir of the Craft*, "The space can be humble ... and it really needs only one thing: a door you are willing to shut. The closed door is your way of telling the world that you mean business."

For Karen, her studio is a space where she can retreat to without the disruption of her inbox, phone or other people. Some people may find it lonely, but she finds it highly inspiring and vastly productive. She is able to create a flow state quickly and easily when she is able to shut the door, become fully engaged in her passion-filled craft and free herself from the bevy of distractions that torment most of us daily.

When it comes to flow, it isn't only about challenging yourself but finding the balance of the challenge with your abilities. For Karen, a former CPA, working as a metalsmith is a challenge in and of itself. It is a craft and one that she continues to develop and refine over time. She clearly has the skills but she continues to challenges herself with different designs and ways of creating jewelry that isn't conventional. Although she creates one-of-kind pieces and small batches of specific pieces, she knows that if she had to create the same piece a thousand times over, it would be a total bore. She wouldn't be challenged and she would lose the flow state that makes her creative process so enjoyable.

Another important condition to create flow is immediate and external feedback. If it took years to get feedback from a particular task or project, you might find it difficult to stay adequately engaged. For Karen in her state of flow, there is constant and immediate feedback. She gets feedback when a clasp doesn't work or if a segment needs to be soldered or whether a necklace just didn't turn out the way she envisioned. Something either works or it doesn't. She also gets immediate feedback when it all comes together and she has a completed piece. She has the immediate feedback throughout the process that makes the flow state more attainable.

Besides the residual effects of getting important tasks done, research has shown that flow is also good for your health. Being in a flow state stimulates you intellectually, emotionally, and spiritually and it's been shown to be physically restorative. When you go into flow, your brains waves reflect a state of calm and are free of anxiety. This alpha state, which operates at 8-14 Hz verses standard waking state of 14-38 Hz, has restorative qualities. So not only are you accomplishing major tasks, but you're also rejuvenating your body and mind. That alone is worth looking further into to find areas of your life and business that produces flow.

Challenge: Prepping To Get Into Flow

Do you know when you're in flow? Do you know what sparks this optimal state?

When was the last time you got lost for hours in an activity?

Did you know it when it was happening? Or, did you realize after the fact that you were in flow? Do you seek out opportunities to flow in your work?

Take a look at the criteria below and see what activities in your business might encourage flow states. Now, schedule time on your calendar to get into flow.

1. Clear, attainable yet stretch goals
2. Intrinsic motivation built into the task
3. Ability to concentrate on a particular topic
4. Ability to challenge you and your skills
5. Immediate feedback

Dial Into Discipline

> "You can't cross a sea by merely staring into the water."
> —Rabindranath Tagore

Creative types and entrepreneurs – which are usually one in the same – are not fond of the topic of discipline. They fear it will stifle their creativity or produce too much structure reminiscent of corporate days. Discipline need not be rigid. Discipline coupled with practice are two keys to getting things done. Even though they may not use the term discipline, successful entrepreneurs realize that self-discipline and focus is what has helped create success.

Practice may seem like an odd concept to bring up while discussing business, but practice implies there is engagement by an individual – a commitment – to a daily exercise with a focused intention. You're not just showing up to punch in and out; you're showing up to gain mastery in your field or to accomplish a goal you've set for yourself. If you were a professional athlete, you'd show up for practice each and every day and work towards a goal of improving your time, getting stronger, working more cohesively with your team and, hopefully, moving one step closer to winning a particular competition or prize. You don't just show up, throw on your uniform and aimlessly throw a ball around or worse, sit on the bench texting with your friends about last night's episode of *Downton Abbey*. You show up focused and ready to better your skills and your game.

With your business, there is a level of practice in professionalism. You show up every day to move yourself and your business towards a particular goal. Your aim is to create and sell an exceptional product or service or impact a significant amount of people with your offering. Although today may be a day that you're feeling under the weather or you didn't get adequate sleep, you still suit up and show up on the field. Because ultimately, it's about the big game.

It takes discipline to show up each day for your own business. Especially if you're starting your business alone or from your home. It is easy to get distracted by family, TV, Internet or even the laundry. In the quiet moments of your day, you may be tempted to wander about, but it's important that you create discipline in your daily practice.

Discipline can be quite individual. Similar to time-management techniques you'll have to find a system and strategy that works best for you. For many people, creating "block time" is essential for getting things done. With block time, you schedule chunks of time on your calendar – essentially setting an appointment with yourself – where you focus on particular tasks or projects. You minimize distractions and keep to your commitment. When you give yourself a specific time frame, you're more inclined to get the tasks done that you've assigned for that time, rather than having a to-do list that you tackle over a course of a day.

Sally McGraw, founder of Already Pretty, freelance journalist, and style and body image writer, shared that routine and structure is critical, "I block off time for absolutely everything, big and small. I'll chunk off four to five hours for bigger projects but also put half-hour tasks on my schedule so they won't be overlooked." For Sally she finds that putting everything on her calendar keeps her on track as well.

For Sarah Von Bargen, founder of the lifestyle blog Yes and Yes, believes that consistently is key to becoming successful. Attributing some of her own consistency to her Type-A personality, Virgo sign, and Germanic heritage, she values her hardworking work-ethic. She has been blogging for five years and hasn't missed a deadline yet. Even when she was traveling the world for ten months, she scheduled all her posts out so she didn't miss a beat with her fans. She believes being consistent, reliable and trustworthy is crucial. Her requirements for her blog are all self-imposed but she is disciplined in showing up for herself and for her audience. This discipline translates into a loyal, loving fan base.

For those also working at home, it is crucial to create some structure around your work day. Perhaps you take a shower and put on street clothes (rather than stay in your jammies) so that you feel a sense that you've started your day. You may also want to schedule an hour at the gym or a yoga class like you would have when you were at a nine-to-five job.

In his book, *Outliers*, Malcolm Gladwell uses the 10,000 Hour Rule to talk about mastery in a field. Based on research by psychologist Anders Ericsson, now at Florida State University, the rule states that a mere 10,000 hours of dedicated practice in your particular field is sufficient to bring about mastery. That may seem like a lot of time – and, it is – but the focus here is on regularly showing up. However, you must not just mindlessly go through the motions but create a focused, intentional practice. So as you work towards practicing your craft and creating discipline for yourself, make sure you are intentional in what you're creating. If you're going to put in the time, it might as well be towards what you ideally desire. The golfer Ben Hogan once said, "Every day you don't practice you're one day further from being good."

Discipline is also a fantastic way to manage and quiet that wicked little ego. In his book, *Infinite Self*, Stuart Wilde shares how he created a disciplined practice to quiet his mental chatter. He committed to getting up at 4 a.m. every day to take a walk in the woods near his home before he started his work day. Rain or shine, hungover or well-rested, he committed to this daily ritual. You can imagine the internal battles that must have raged on mornings where he would have rather turned over and pushed snooze for a few more hours.

In her book, *The Creative Habit*, Twyla Tharp, outlines the need for habits when it comes to creating. A life-long dancer and accomplished choreographer, she believes that creativity is enhanced when we are self-disciplined. At seventy-two years young, Tharp rises each day at 5:30 a.m. She throws on her workout clothes, walks out of her Manhattan home and hails a cab to her gym. She spends the next two hours working out. As she explains, "The ritual is not the stretching and weight training I put my body through each morning at the gym; the ritual is the cab. The moment I tell the driver where to go I have completed my ritual." She knows that once she's in the cab, she is committed to going to the gym, and the hardest part done. This habit – this ritual – is a practice in self-discipline. The mind may become noisy, but when you press through the chatter and keep moving, then you'll find yourself accomplishing things you'd never expected.

For you, your ritual might be showing up at your desk every morning at exactly 8:30 a.m. with a cup of coffee in hand. Or, it may be that you speak to your business partner at 7:00 a.m. every work day to discuss what you plan to accomplish. Decide what your ritual might be and then stick to it. Self discipline in one area of your life will end up benefitting all areas of your life as well. When you show up for yourself, you show up for others, too.

It's particularly important to establish rituals early on in your business. They may change over time, but creating good habits early will serve you well. As Tharp shares, "It's vital to establish some rituals – automatic but decisive patterns of behavior – at the beginning of the creative process, when you are most at peril of turning back, chickening out, giving up, or going the wrong way."

Through creating rituals similar to the examples above, you tell your ego, "I'm in charge." You can create this ritual in your private life and it will carry over into your business as well, although it's wise to create habits in all areas of your life. The ego soon realizes that it no longer runs the show as you move towards the bold goals you've set for yourself in your work and life.

As Whitney Kell, a wildly successful health and business coach, summed up nicely, "The reason most people are not successful is that they don't do the work. They make mistakes and when things get uncomfortable they give up. If you are willing to make lots of mistakes and view them as lessons verses failures and then ask yourself three questions 'What went well?' 'What did I learn?' 'What will I do differently next time?', then apply the lesson and take action you will move towards what you want. Most people give up right before they are about to break through." Don't be the majority of people who either don't take action or stop only steps before the finish line. Often the most challenging and difficult part of the journey is mere moments before a major success. So hang tight, keep taking focused action and stay the course. You'll be glad you did.

Spotlight: Ursula Mentjes -
From Farm Girl to Sales Star

Looking at Ursula now, you'd never guess she grew up on a farm in rural Minnesota. It was a community of domestic violence, and although she loves her parents, she decided to leave home at 15 years old to get a job. She worked her way through college at St. Olaf's with a plan to go to law school. Upon graduating, she quickly realized that she couldn't afford to pay for an advanced degree, so instead, she decided to move to Boulder, Colorado with a friend. While working as a retail clerk for Pier 1 Imports, she struck up a conversation with a woman who offered her a job for an international computer consulting company. She jumped at the opportunity. As a sales associate, she had to make one hundred sales calls each day before going home, which was grueling but a practice in itself of discipline. She quickly became a rising star, and with her sights set on becoming the CEO one day, Ursula was ask to take over a branch that was losing over $60,000 a month. She quickly turned the failing branch around and it soon sold $3M in just one month. She stayed focused on her goal of becoming CEO and within a few shorts years, at the age of 27, she became the CEO of a $20M company.

But that wasn't enough for Ursula. She left the corporate world and started her own consulting firm in 2004 that specializes in working with entrepreneurs and sales professionals. One of her keys to success and her advice for other entrepreneurs is to be disciplined with your time. She shared, "Challenges will come up but you must be disciplined and persevere to get it off the ground." She often speaks to audiences about how it's important to stay focused and to create one clear and focused goal in order to shift your business. As entrepreneurs, we often get distracted by all our ideas and we flit around trying this or that idea and never seeing on idea through. She lives by the principle of self-discipline and it's working well for her and for her clients.

Spotlight: Jenee Dana: On Finding Fun in Getting Things Done

Jenee Dana, founder of Focus Opus, knew that creating a practice of discipline was imperative for her to be successful and design the life she craved. While in her second year at UCLA, Jenee was seriously considering dropping out of college. She was getting good grades but was increasingly unhappy. Her physical body was showing the signs of burnout, breaking out in hives and eczema. To make matters worse she was also diagnosed with ADHD which came as both a surprise and a relief. Instead of dropping out she decided to condense her last two years and finish at the end of her third year which is fairly unheard of in most academic institutions but especially at a UC.

Most students at UCLA were lucky to finish within five years. She studied productivity principles by several experts and reversed engineered what it would take to achieve her goals. The system she developed worked like a charm and she was able to graduate that third year while holding down a job and managing an active social life. The icing on the cake: she was the happiest she had been in years. It took discipline and thoughtful planning but she knew it was possible. Her health and happiness was dependent on it. Now, she shares her secrets with college students who want to do the same as well as business people who want to get the most out of their day. "It can be fun to get it done," Jenee shared with enthusiasm. "But first you have to stop managing your time. Time management is not effective. Defining your values and priorities comes first." Jenee believes that by discovering what you value and then tackling your projects and tasks from that place of understanding you are able to be highly productive.

Challenge: Discipline, Practice and Ritual

What are your feelings toward self-discipline?

Do you believe it's necessary, or do you prefer to be "creative" and ignore the call of keeping yourself on track?

What areas of your life are lacking discipline?

What areas of your life are rocking it with self-discipline?

What rituals can you establish in your work life?

What small practices can you incorporate every day to keep you moving steadily forward with your business?

What rituals or practices will you commit to daily or weekly?

You may be wondering why there are so many quotes about fishing and the sea in this chapter. There is a power and mystery that comes with the ocean. It is vast, there are many unknowns that may arise along the way, and you rely on internal navigating systems to maneuver about the ocean. There is always a certain risk when going out to sea. Perhaps a storm hits that capsizes your vessel or you get off course and end up in Jamaica verses Japan. You may be alone or have a small team on your boat. There may be times of infighting or even a mutiny. So much can go wrong. Yet, so much can go right. Along your journey, you discover new lands, you meet new people, you learn to rely on your team, and you push yourself physically and emotionally. You discover more about yourself than if had you stayed on land casting a longing gaze out to sea. You may find beautiful treasures or simply have treasured moments. You feel accomplished, confident and maybe even a bit worn out. But your fatigue is from experiencing the exhilarating feat of piloting a mighty ship through unknown waters. And, you realize you're a better person for the adventure.

Inspiration Library

Music
New Shoes by Paolo Nutini
Empire State of Mind by Jay-Z
Imma Be by Black Eyed Peas
I'm Coming Out by Diana Ross

Movies
Slumdog Millionaire
Silver Linings Playbook
Julie & Julia

Books
Flow: The Psychology of Optimal Experiences by Mihaly Csikszentmihalyi
The Creative Habit: Learn It and Use It for Life by Twyla Tharp
Wealthy Spirit: Daily Affirmations for Financial Stress Reduction by Chellie Campbell
Infinite Self: 33 Steps to Reclaiming Your Inner Power by Stuart Wilde
Life Is a Verb: 37 Days to Wake Up, Be Mindful, and Live Intentionally by Patti Digh
Do More Great Work: Stop the Busywork: Start The Work That Matters by Michael Bungay Stainer

Chapter 6

Get Connected (Community)

"There is a special place in hell for women who don't help other women."
—Madeleine Albright (Keynote speech at Celebrating Inspiration luncheon with the WNBA's All-Decade Team, 2006)"

Although we're social, communal creatures, women have a tendency to go it alone when it comes to business. This is an area where networking, building teams, leading groups, chatting up people at the playground, having drinks with friends, and general socializing really pays off. Yet this is an area many women find themselves deficient in.

Look, you can't venture this road alone. In the last few chapters, we've been working on the inner work that needs to be in place to get you off and running. Now it's time to reach out, connect, network, socialize, team up, lead, ask for help, make coffee dates, find mentors, get coaching and give back.

This is also the fun part. You're going to be connecting with so many amazing, smart, and wise people while creating a community of support and serving the world. So don't shy away from creating a bigger business for yourself because you're uncomfortable asking for help or because you don't like networking. Success is definitely a team sport. Surround yourself with high quality people, attract your perfect customers, get your family and friends on board and get out there.

Business Partners and Teams

Like so many others, Alexis Maybank rode the wave of the dot-com boom and bust, spending four years helping to build eBay. She had wanted to start her own company, but her first venture ended up being a flop. It failed not because the idea wasn't sound but because the partnership never gelled to form a cohesive company. Alexis was looking for her next venture and found it in a business that was just getting off the ground called FirstLook. She was asked to come on to help form and lead the company. After her previous founder experience, where she learned the valuable lesson that execution and partnership is much more important that an idea, she was much more careful in terms of the people she would partner with. Even though she clearly had the skills to run a technology company, FirstLook was aiming to be a luxury brand teaming up with fashion luminaries such as Versace, Valentino and Dolce & Gabbana. She needed someone who could navigate that world and who had a rolodex of contacts to get them off and running. Alexis had one person in mind, and it happened to be a dear friend and former classmate, Alexandra Wilkis Wilson. Alexandra was working at Bulgaria at the time after a stint in financial services. When Alexis, in her yoga pants, walked into the posh Bulgari store to chat with Alexandra about the opportunity, the one thing that concerned her wasn't whether she'd be open to the opportunity but whether it would strain their relationship if things didn't work out. But for Alexis, now a mother of two, the risk was one she was willing to take. The risk paid off. The business and friendship grew into Gilt Groupe, a company valued at over $1 billion.

What Alexis learned from her first venture was the importance of choosing the right partner and creating a team that she could trust and that complemented one another's skills. Further, it was crucial that they genuinely respected and liked one another.

In their book, *By Invitation Only*, Alexis Maybank and Alexandra Wilkis Wilson provide a checklist for deciding upon whether to partner with someone.

This handy checklist includes:

1. Have you seen your partner handle difficult situations?
2. Do you want the same things for your company?
3. Do you have similar energies and work ethic?
4. How do you fight?
5. Is there any doubt or red flag... any?
6. Do you have complementary personalities?
7. Is your partner an upper or a downer?

When partnering with someone it is important that you ask yourself these questions and have an open conversation with the person you're going to go into business with. Partnership is very similar to marriage and you need to know what you're getting yourself into. It's also important you hash out your needs, wants and ways of working so that as things come up you're able to sit and talk openly and frankly.

For Jadah Sellner her road to partnership was unexpected. She had planned to start a parenting education website on her own and had done all the necessary legwork to get started. Then she was reintroduced to someone she had met seven years earlier at a mommy's group in Los Angeles. Both women had since moved from L.A.: Jadah having moved to Hawaii then to Northern California and Jen Hansard having moved to Florida. Although resistant to teaming up because as she put it "its hard when it's your idea baby," she saw the benefit of bringing on someone with Jen's skills. Jadah and Jen partnered up and switched gears from parenting education to green smoothies and launched the wildly successful site, Simply Green Smoothies. Jadah shared that each woman brings a different skill set to the table but their core values are very similar. Jadah brings the online marketing and community building piece while Jen brings the design and branding focus. They both know their strengths and contribution and continue to divide and conquer based on their individual offerings. Based on the success of their partnership and their business (their business is able to support two families), Jadah encourages others to partner up if they find someone who complements them and who they can trust.

For Whitney Moss and Heather Flett, they were close friends long before they forged a working partnership. They each had their first child within months of one another and as a result of this major life transition began writing down lists of things they'd come across being new moms, activities to do and experiences they shared. These lists became their first blog and within six month got picked up by larger bloggers. "It was all innocent and natural enough," Whitney shared about starting the blog and the partnership over eight years. Their business has grown into two popular blogs, 510Families.com and RookieMoms.com and a book *The Rookie Mom's Handbook: 250 Activities to do with (and without!) your baby.* Heather has spoken to several women about how to create a successful partnership, "People worry they are giving up too much control. When we go out on our own – motivated by our passions – we wonder 'how will another person possibly care as much as I do about it?'" This is a reasonable concern and one to address with yourself and with your potential partner. Although close friends, they drew up a partnership agreement early on that defined the parameters of their partnership including who does what and the division of profits. "Don't be afraid to revisit it often," Heather recommended. Recently, they found that when questions arose around individual consulting assignments, instead of trying to figure it out again, the answers actually were found in their original agreement.

Spotlight: Laura Slezinger On
Something Ventured

Laura Slezinger became a lawyer at probably the worst time in recent history. She finished her second law degree (the first being her J.D. and a second, a LL.M. in Intellectual Property & Technology Law) in early 2009 and descending on the job market when law firms were dissolving left and right. No one was hiring associates let alone ones fresh out of law school and agencies were contracting "temp lawyers" for $10-$15 hours basically what one would make working at Starbucks. It was a difficult time but it didn't stop Laura. She had been involved with Girls in Tech, a non-profit that has a purpose of engaging, educating and empowering influential women in technology, for several years and was surrounded by women taking the leap into starting their own companies. "How can I be a voice for this organization and be afraid of being an entrepreneur? If I'm championing women who take risks in business then I need to take risks as well." Laura continued, "I've been surrounded by stories of entrepreneurs and everyone says how they never felt equipped to start" and as a result she realized she too could start a business and take the leap. She and her business partner were introduced by mutual friends. Nnena Ukuku founder of Black Founder's Startup Ventures and Laura were both involved in promoting people under represented in both technology and business and they found that they could team up to build something great. "We hit if off right away. I just wanted to get to know her better," Laura shared. As a result, Venture Gained Legal, a boutique law practice in San Francisco was born. She revealed their success as partners: "We have shared values. Our values and our mission are in alignment. I respect her and she respects me. We can disagree and have honest conversations about it.

> Our central values never are in question, it's more about implementation and the route we take." Although she described herself as a highly independent person she said that her partnership has been a real blessing. When people are solo they don't have the opportunity to discuss ideas and have a sounding board to bounce ideas off of. You also may not have the emotional support that a partnership provides. As Laura expressed, "When I feel discouraged, she can pick me up and vice-versa."

When you're building your team it is critical to be thoughtful about who you bring in. This goes for those you hire as contractors or others you may partner with. Nothing can cause more strain on your life as a bad partnership, an inappropriate hire or dysfunctional working relationship. Who you bring into your business will be a direct reflection of your company's values – and your values. You wouldn't want to bring on someone who is disrespectful of others or who doesn't share your work ethic. Take the time upfront to be highly selective in who you bring on as your team. By taking the extra effort upfront you will save hours of headache and difficultly down the road.

It may seem daunting to build a team and often it's advised to get help and coaching on how to manage people. This became painfully true for Chantal Pierrat who wasn't afraid to share that she hasn't always led from a place of what she refers to as "feminine power". In fact, there was a lot of unlearning she had to go through to get to where she is today both personally and professionally. While getting her MBA, she learned that drive, competitiveness and aggression were how you got things done. She used these skills in one of her roles and it did not go over very well. She was brought into a company, prior to launching her own, to help turn things around and the culture reacted negatively to her more masculine way of doing business – what she called "working like a dude." She felt like she had to protect her rightness. Thankfully through coaching and reflecting, she was able to find ways to connect, collaborate and work much better with her team. As of result of her own personal turnaround, the business doubled. The results were much better than expected and with a lot less effort. And, after her second baby was born, people were incredibly helpful when she came back from maternity leave. "As women we look around at how we compromise ourselves. We're fearful that our value won't be recognized. What if we're not big, driven and bold. But our best work is done from a place of magic and giving."

Her mission is to foster and promote true connection, collaboration and feminine leadership through her Emerging Women Live events which aim to support and propel this emerging movement. She has realized the power and beauty in women connecting and how we can help each other lead from a stronger more authentic place.

Spotlight: Cat Lincoln On Valuing People

Cat Lincoln not only has a strong belief in herself but has an even stronger belief that the best work is done in a truly collaborative environment. Growing up professionally on the corporate track she landed incredible female mentors all along her journey. Women would not only recognized her for her skills and potential but would fight to get her titles, promotions and money. It didn't happen just once but time and again she worked for supportive women leaders. One of her mentors gave her great advice when it came to managing teams that she still uses to this day, "You're not managing people, you're coaching them."

When it came time to make the leap and start her own firm she knew the value of great people and a collaborative culture. She partnered up with three other women and co-founded Clever Girls Collective, a social media agency offering content marketing and native advertising at scale. As a company, Clever Girls "found success in acknowledging who we are and what we do well." She believes and fosters the notion that the only way the company wins is to win as a team. And, you see this in action when people happily pitch in on projects even when it's outside their job function.

For Cat, her favorite day of the year is when she is giving out raises, bonuses, promotions or recognition. She feels like she is able to pay it back for all the years she has received invaluable support from others and for acknowledging those who help make her company a success.

She knows that her staff of eighteen relies on the partners to run the company well and she doesn't take that responsibility lightly but they do still have fun in the office. She shared how after a three-hour highly productive meeting they jumped on the computer to look at faux leather jackets at Forever21. For Cat, her partners and their team live the adage, "Work hard and play hard" with a dose of clever fun.

Your Tribe

"Keep away from people who belittle your ambitions. Small people always do that, but the really great make you feel that you, too, can become great."
— Mark Twain

Regardless of whether you choose to build a team, partner up with someone else or go it solo, it's important that you build a tribe that supports you. Your tribe might include peers in complementary businesses, other business owners, joint venture partners, mentors, an accountant, contractors, customer service reps, a printer, other vendors, a web designer, investors, a coach, advisors, a virtual assistant, board of directors, a hypnotherapist, an acupuncturist, a personal trainer, a nanny, or a dog-walker. Your tribe includes everyone that enables you to run your business in the most efficient, healthy and prosperous way possible. As you'll notice, each one of the people listed you can explicitly chose. You can create standards of integrity to filter them through and weed out any and all people who you don't mix well with. And always, always trust your gut when you're interviewing. Your gut is very wise and won't steer you wrong. It's important to know that you have people who have your back and you can rely on to keep you and your business running smoothly.

Alison Bailey Vercruysse, founder of 18 Rabbits, a company focused on healthy granola and granola bar products, originally thought that being an entrepreneur was all about the money. Having worked at the Federal Reserve Bank of Chicago and earning an MBA may have something to do with that. But when Alison started a company based on her passion and newfound profession as professional baker, she realized it wasn't just about the numbers. "It's not about the money, it's really about the people. Now I focus on the people and I attract the right ones to help build my vision," said Alison.

For Erika Bloom, of Erika Bloom Pilates in New York City, "embracing the community" has created a wonderful network and a lot of trust. This trust is something that you can only build when you value your tribe and they in turn value the work you do.

Your tribe also includes your customers and clients. It's important to surround yourself with the type of people you want to work with. They will energize you. You will also better serve them because you will know exactly what they need and want and you love giving it to them. Yes, you can choose who you do business with and "fire" anyone who you don't want to work with. Here is yet another application of the old 80-20 Rule. This is the widely applied principle that divides the meaningful from the less important into 80 and 20 percent. For our purposes 80 percent of your complaints and issues come from 20 percent of your customers. That 20 percent are also your biggest critics, will demand the most of you and your time, and are simply a huge pain in the ass to work with. So fire them. Let them go. Let someone else serve them and serve them better. It's not worth the effort when the majority of your easy-going clients and the ones you prefer to serve are getting less of you because you're bending over backwards for the troublesome ones. You deserve better and you deserve to work with the people you want to work with. Isn't that one reason you went into business for yourself?

Shawne Duperon, six-time EMMY Award winner, best-selling author and founder of Shawne TV, has interviewed many of the recent US presidents and hundreds of famous celebrities. She is currently producing on an inspiring documentary about forgiveness. Over the last twenty years, she has worked with a variety of interesting, fascinating and, I'm guessing, challenging people. She shared her favorite aspect of being an entrepreneur and a word of warning, "In essence, whether we're conscious of it or not, we pick the people we're working with. I consciously choose my business partners and clients. If you have sucky clients, you drew them in." She purposefully draws in the people she wants to work with and it's reflective on her life. "There is joy and happiness in my world. I'm moved by what I do every single day. I get to work with the most amazing people," said Shawne.

Is there really a separation between your business and personal life? Not really, especially when you're running your own show. Your business can be all-consuming and you easily bring it home with you – if you're not already running it from your home. You are often excited to share your experiences with your personal tribe: your significant other, family, friends and friendly acquaintances. You cannot always chose your family, but you can chose what you will listen to and what you will ignore. You can choose how much advice to heed and how much to toss in the trash. Often your family means well and is looking out for your best interest, but sometimes, you may be a reminder of the chances they passed by, the risks they were too afraid to take or their business ideas that never saw the light of day. There may be jealously that is at an unconscious level and they may lash out at you in undeserving ways. Find a way to manage those relationships, either by having a frank conversation or by creating some distance. You may not control how others behave towards you but you can control how you react to them. In some cases the envy may have nothing to do with you and everything to do with them – unless, of course, their money is involved. If they have invested in your business, you will have to have a different conversation involving how much input they ought to have. This similar scenario may also come up with friends who are happy for you but who wish they had the courage to go out on their own.

As Shawne eluded to, the relationships in your life are consciously or unconsciously chosen by you. The relationships and people you draw into your life are reflecting aspects of you. People act as a mirror so check in with yourself and ask why you've attracted these relationships into your life and why you continue to foster them. If you need to make some changes, now is the time.

Jess Butcher, founder of the UK technology company Blipper, shared, "Another, possibly slightly strange piece of advice — but if you haven't already got one, find a good better half or at least draw closer to those real friends in your life whose support you'll need. The life of an entrepreneur is all-consuming, with a poor work-life balance and a roller coaster of highs and lows. Having one personal, special cheerleader who celebrates your highs with you and brings you out of despondency during the lows makes all the difference and keeps you focused and balanced."

For Elizabeth Dehn of Beauty Bets and One Love Organics her husband has been one of her biggest champions. After several years working for big retailers and always considering herself "a corporate girl for life" she decided to branch out on her own. In support of his wife's dreams, Elizabeth's husband incorporated her as a Christmas gift. He also reminds her that everything is a series of choices and if you don't like something you can always choose something else. Great advice.

Many women who have husbands or life partners noted the importance of that relationship and how the emotional support is invaluable to their success. A few women took the relationship one step further: they chose to launch a business with their husbands or brought them on as the business grew. Your spouse is often your greatest champion and yet someone who is easy to take for granted. As you start and grow your business, make sure you take the time to communicate openly about your dreams, goals and what you need. Opening up the conversation early on will ensure a free flowing line of communication as things inevitably change and grow.

Your tribe will also include your mentors and, of course, your mentors-in-absentia – your role models. There is a lot of talk in the media about the importance of mentors. They can open doors, make introductions, act as a champion, show you the quickest path, help you avoid pitfalls and be a sounding board for ideas. It is important to find people who you connect with who are a few steps, a few years, or even a few decades ahead of you on this path.

I know you wish you could just go to a website and locate a mentor, like a dating service, but it isn't that easy. It requires a bit of work and sometimes some clever uncovering to find one that suits you. But it's worth the work to find one.

Shaherose Charania's biggest obstacle when she first started her company was admittedly herself. She was definitely getting in her own way with thoughts of, "How dare I help people *and* make money," she openly shared. This belief was difficult to release but thankfully a mentor helped her overcome this mental block that was holding her back. Besides being a founder of an early stage incubator for mobile ideas, she has also created a successful media company which is helping women in technology. Women2.0 focuses on women, technology and entrepreneurship and provides a valuable platform for women in technology to learn, connect and be inspired by one another.

Jennifer Ferguson is on her third company, Symphony Financial, and attributes part of her success to having valuable mentors along the way. "I became successful much faster as a result," she shared. Many of her business role models were also her mentors in the financial services arena. Jennifer knows the importance of establishing a strong tribe. With her latest company, rather than the standard transactional business she was accustomed to, she wanted to surround herself with great people by assembling a best-in-class team. She also wanted to serve a smaller amount of clients at a higher, more personal level and create a team that serves them by covering all aspects of their finances, from insurance to stocks and investments. She has created a model that builds a tribe that she loves. Knowing how influential her mentors have been on her success and believing in the power of giving back, she is also an avid mentor to others.

"Your network is everything," Erin Newkirk shared enthusiastically. She is not short on fantastic mentors and advisors, and when I asked her about other people I should speak with, she gave me a list of many impressive women who she's been lucky enough to have mentor her. Her award-winning company, Red Stamp, is a mobile and social commerce company focused on stylish correspondence. She noted that it may take a while and a bit of hard work to find role models and mentors, but it's invaluable to do so. She advised that when you reach out to people for mentorship, "be sure to give them something in return." Given that Erin's business stems from her love of corresponding and being raised on the importance of thank you cards, she is a savvy user of the law of reciprocity. The law states that people will respond to a positive action with another positive action. In a social situation, it means that in response to a friendly exchange, people will respond in a kinder, more cooperative manner. The law of reciprocity and her enthusiastic personality has been working fantastic for Erin. "If you're providing value for people, mentors will follow," she added.

Often what I hear about mentors is that they believe in the protégé long before the protégé believes in the themselves. When you're starting out and unsure of – well, everything – it's nice to have someone who has faith that you have what it takes to make your dreams a reality.

For many women, an accountability partner or a mastermind group has been a great way to keep them honest and in constant action. An accountability partner is someone you regularly speak to who is on a similar journey. They don't necessarily need to be in a similar type of company, and it can actually be highly beneficial to have someone outside your industry. This differing perspective can open you up to new ideas. It's important, though, that there is consistency and that you keep each other on track with your plans and goals. Partners usually meet, often over the phone, to share what they plan to do for the week and what they've accomplished the week before. When you work alone or with a virtual team, it's refreshing to regularly talk to someone about your business goals and any issues that may have come up. You and your partner also share your weekly, monthly, quarterly and annual goals and ask one another to hold each other accountable. I've heard of people putting money on the line as a way to make sure everyone accomplishes the tasks they set forth for a particular week. If you don't complete your self-assigned task or project, the money is then donated to charity. What a splendid idea. Mastermind groups function in a similar way with a few more people added to the mix. They can be formed informally, or you can find one to join. You share ideas, best practices, what's working for your business and what's not working, share contacts and resources, as well as your aspirations and goals.

There is a fascinating and growing trend that caught the eye of writer Pamela Rykman. She was interviewing high-powered female executives and found that they often had a close knit female power posse supporting them behind the scenes. Women were informally organizing dinner groups, networking groups and salons where they could come together regularly to mix, mingle, support and empower. In her book, *Stiletto Network*, Rykman found that women were uniting to provide guidance, act as sounding boards, and provide support for one another along this common journey. One particular circle included many of the female titans of Silicon Valley who would casually get together at one another's house while children would run around in the background. She found that these circles were also major hubs of business, investing and mentorship. The mentoring relationships ran both ways. The seasoned veterans mentor and invest in younger women's companies and the younger gals share their fresh insights and technical prowess with the veterans. Rykman writes, "Many established women invest in the young ladies' startups thinking they'll bestow wisdom and shape careers. But almost without fail, they end up expounding on what they've gained in return." These are gatherings in which everyone wins. This phenomenon is not only seen in the major economic hubs or in robust industries such as financial services, technology and media. Women are forming similar groups everywhere, in every demographic, industry and stage of their career. "It's about women banding together to achieve their destinies and change the world," says Rykman.

Your tribe is your greatest external asset. The people that you meet and who join you on this journey play a valuable role in your success, growth and happiness. This isn't to be taken lightly. You have a choice as to whom you invite along for this adventure. Choose wisely.

Spotlight: Rebecca Keller's Lessons On Hiring

Rebecca Keller never imagined becoming a CEO of a company, let alone one she founded. She was, first and foremost, an academic wielding an impressive PhD in Biophysical Chemistry. But when she started to have kids, all that changed. She wasn't keen on sending her children to public school and decided to home school them instead. She was frustrated by the lack of resources available, especially in the sciences. As she shared: "Today's science curricula and programs are not teaching kids the basic building blocks for science in a way that will help them understand real chemistry, biology, physics, astronomy and geology. We are a wealthy country and have all the resources we need to do an excellent job educating the next generation, yet our kids are graduating without a basic understanding of real science." She began writing books, not only for her family, but for others as well, and then launched her own publishing house called Gravitas Publishing Inc. that specializes in science education for kids. Currently, her market is home-schooled families, although she is hoping that her books will begin to permeate schools and institutions as well.

Although she called herself "the reluctant CEO," she's finally accepted this role over the last two years. As her company was rapidly growing, she knew she needed to bring on a strong operations person who could also work virtually. She recognized that there was "a huge untapped talent pool of women who wanted to stay at home but who are powerful, brilliant and who would be incredible assets to the right company." She indeed found one of those assets. She brought on a COO with stellar skills who used to work on Wall Street. Although she was making a lot of money, she really wanted to stay home with her kids. Rebecca felt like she hit gold with this hire and her COO was thrilled to be able to work from home for an emerging company. Her whole team works remotely, which can be challenging at times, but they use all the technology available to keep the lines of communication open. Rebecca is amazed at the quality of talented women out there who chose to opt out of the traditional workforce. If you're looking to bring on a team or hire an independent contractor, there are plenty of wonderful options. There is truly a goldmine of talent out there to unearth.

Challenge: Build Your Ideal Tribe

It's important to stop and take a look at the people surrounding you and determine who is adding value and positivity to your life and who is sucking you dry with their cynicism, negativity and potential jealousy. It is vital to clear out the Debbie Downers as much as possible because as you're starting and growing your business, you need as much support and positive energy as possible.

Let's map out your tribe.

Take out a piece of paper and in the middle of the page write ME with a circle around it. From the center circle, add branches similar to a tree. Write out all the people who make up your tribe. If you'd like to use branches for major groupings such as "family," "friends," "community," "peers," "support" and so on, then create leaves off the branches to write down the name of the people associated with that branch.

Now that you see your tribe in visual form, ask yourself:

Who are my biggest supporters?

Who are rolling their eyes at my ideas and at me?

Who brushes off my dreams or ignores me when I share aspects of my business? (It may be as subtle as they change the conversation any time you bring up topics around your business or project.)

Who are key players that are missing from my tribe?

What new tribal members should I be on the lookout for to bring in?

It's time to take charge of your tribe. If you need to shift energy and time away from certain people and seek out new friends and peers, there is no better time than now. You don't necessarily need to end relationships, but you may just need to minimize your contact with them during particular stages of your life and business. If you've discovered that there are people you'd like to add to your tribe, keep a look out and begin to ask for introductions.

Networking

You walk into a large room where people are milling about, looking awkward, wearing name tags and nursing glasses of cheap wine. You scan to see if any faces look remotely familiar, then realize you probably don't know anyone there. You wonder why you attend these events, because often you walk away with a handful of business cards from people who barely stopped to ask your name. After deciding to stay, you slap on your obligatory paper name tag, grab a glass of wine and hope that when you turn around someone friendly will chat with you. Another evening passes, one that could have been spent with your family or friends or even catching up on your DVR recordings, and you wonder, *was it worth it?*

Networking can be a drag. When I started my acupuncture practice, I was a networking junkie. Since I didn't have many patients, my full time job was attending Chamber of Commerce mixers, meeting people for coffee, going to weekly networking meetings, and attending cocktail parties. I was working the circuit because I needed to build my business – and fast. However, I had no strategy at all. Often the events I attended involved people pushing cards at one another and speaking to you with one eye over your shoulder, plotting who to speak to next. Sometimes when people would find out I was an acupuncturist, they would move on quickly, not seeing any money to be made on me.

There were many things I learned that first year. The first lesson is to show genuine interest in the person you're speaking with by actively listening and making eye contact. As they're talking, imagine they're the only person in the room. Ask them questions — and not only about their business. Find out where they're originally from, or what's the last movie they watched. It doesn't have to be all work-related chitchat. And often people appreciate this casual exchange over the staid conversation around your profession.

Secondly, have a strategy. I attended several conferences over the last few years, some attracting over five hundred attendees. It's easy to make brief introductions and move on to the next person. After attending one large four-day conference where I met many people, I walked away thinking that I really didn't make any deep or significant connections. I even followed up with everyone I spoke to and only a few responded out of courtesy. After learning from that event, I decided that the following conference would be different. As I was driving to another four-day long event with four hundred in attendance, I set a specific intention. I told myself that I would meet two people and really get to know them. Rather than quantity, I was going to focus on quality. I was going to refrain from flitting around and changing seats after every break as we were encouraged to do, and I would sit with them and develop a deeper connection. And, voilà, that is exactly what I did. I met two amazing women early on in the conference and we've stayed in contact ever since.

When it comes to networking, you need to turn your thinking around. Networking is not about how others can help you, it is about how you can help others. Who can you introduce them to? How can you help their business? How can you support their cause? When you walk into a room thinking, *how can I help* rather than *what's in it for me*, it changes not only your perspective on an otherwise tedious exchange, but people will be drawn to you as well.

The law of reciprocity comes alive in these exchanges. If you are nice and giving to others, they will most likely be kind in response. Keep in mind, you're not manipulating a situation and being nice purely for the sense of getting something in return. Your intention is to genuinely help others and if, in the end, it comes back to you, then all the better.

It was a grueling first year in business – made even more challenging because I was pregnant at the time. I also wouldn't trade it for the world. I ended up meeting amazing people and my closest business friends are women I met attending these events. We were drawn to one another, not because of our businesses, but our genuine interest in getting to know one another. We became friends, clients to one another, partners on projects, and each other's biggest cheerleaders. A few of us even formed a mastermind group that is still going strong today.

Sometimes, when it comes to networking, you need a little shove. Randy Peyser, founder of Author One Stop, got pushed into learning some networking strategies from her mentor. Twelve years ago, she was at a book expo in New York City. Her mentor, Jill Lublin, was on stages every week giving speeches and was comfortable working a room, but for Randy, this was new territory. The conference was packed with people — over thirty thousand in attendance — and "everyone was going a mile a minute," Randy recalled. She knew she wanted to speak to the press, and when she saw some bigwigs from particular media outlets, she realized it was her chance. She wanted to go speak to them but she had what she calls a "hiccup of hesitation." Jill, knowing Randy wanted to approach them, pushed her to overcome her fear and resistance and encouraged her to walk up to them and introduce herself. The rest of the conference, Jill would say, "Media person. Go!" and Randy would run over and speak to them. We forget that certain people, due to their profession or fancy title, are still people just like us. Often, we're hesitant to speak to new people or ask for what we want. But how are you ever going to meet anyone if you don't take the chance? Jill also gave Randy the advice to attend four new networking events every month rather than just revisiting the same ones over and over. As Randy shared, "Keep showing up. Connections are built over time and the more you show up, the more people will get to know you and trust you."

I would take that advice one step further. To be successful in networking, it's important to show up but with intention, a thoughtful strategy and a focus on how you can serve others. As women, we tend to like to build deep relationships rather than superficial ones, so take the time and energy it takes to foster these relationships. Do what comes naturally to us and meaningfully connect. Networking can be more enjoyable if you take a different spin on it.

Maria Johnson, De Novo Legal PC is one skilled networker. She learned it early on when her father took her to Europe on business and she watched his deal-making skills firsthand with clients. She never quite knew what he was doing but through observing his interactions with affluent individuals, she was nonetheless influenced. Maria took these skills into law school and beyond as she maneuvered her way through the entertainment industry. When she shared her story (sorry ladies, details are purposefully vague because of the people she works with) it was clear that relationships are the cornerstone to her success. Her entire career is saturated with stories of connection, introductions, relationships and networking. Her own practice which is a unique blend of legal services and creative brand management has thrived solely on word of mouth. She values her network and shared that she has never lost touched with anyone she has met along the way. Every year she sends out holiday cards to a list of approximately four hundred people in her network because she believes it's important to remind people that they've touched your life in some way. Maria, a mother of three who is married to a fellow entrepreneur, has not stopped with just her legal consulting firm. She is also heavily involved in two other international product-based companies both of which are growing rapidly. Her ability to meet people along the way, value each person she meets, and consistently and authentically stay in touch with them is a model for how networking is successfully done.

Successful entrepreneurs are great networkers, but it isn't always in the traditional definition of the word. They're excellent people-persons and they value relationships, both new and old. They seek out new opportunities to grow their existing networks and are also open to meeting a variety of different and diverse individuals. Business is not a solo sport. It is a team sport, and it's time to go out and start recruiting.

Spotlight: Charmaine Hammond
On Tribe and Asking

Charmaine Hammond is a consultant, author and speaker who started her career as a Correctional Officer working in adult and youth institutions, and later managing young offender facilities in Canada. She knows a thing or two about people. She eventually became a Contract Negotiation Specialist for the Canadian government. When she decided to branch out on her own in 1997, she and her husband were living in a small community. She recalled her biggest obstacle as "rebranding yourself in a community where they see you in a specific role."

Hers was a town of only one hundred thousand people that didn't have a big entrepreneurial community. She managed for eight years not having the support of other entrepreneurs. She later moved to Edmonton, Alberta, which dramatically helped her business. What she discovered along the way is the importance "in getting really comfortable with the ask early on. You will avoid costly mistakes and it helps prevent stress," said Charmaine.

Charmaine believes it builds confidence and a certain level of openness when you keep asking for help and, as she put it, "It doesn't cost anything." Her husband has now joined the company. "Many entrepreneurs don't have the level of support from their partner. Some husbands don't see the business as a "real" business and they don't think she needs the time. Finding a way to work with your spouse, and engage their talents and expertise in the business can lead to stronger relationships and business. It took my husband and I quite a while to figure out how to work effectively together in business, and when we learned to capitalize on each other's strengths, and separate business from marriage, our relationship and business went to a whole new level of great!" she shared.

Charmaine is lucky her husband is supportive and a great asset to the company. He's helpful in both listening to her vent as well as solving problems, but she has to be clear which hat he is to wear. "With my husband, when I talk about business, I am clear when I begin whether I want to vent, have him help me solve a problem, or just brainstorm," she shared. She also learned a valuable lesson on asking when she finished writing her book, *On Toby's Terms*, which has since been a best-seller and has been optioned for a movie. She has admired Jack Canfield for years (having also attended his workshops) and wanted to ask him to endorse her book. She optimistically reached out to him via email. Some days later, she received an email back from what she imagined was an assistant saying that he wasn't interested. Disappointed, she took the email to her husband to see what she may have said that didn't quite work. He took one look at it and told her that it didn't sound anything like Charmaine. She rewrote it in her own authentic, heartfelt voice and within seven minutes of pressing send she received a message directly from Jack saying he'd be happy to endorse the book. For Charmaine, *the ask* had to come from her heart rather than her head, and with that authentic voice, she got exactly what she wanted.

Asking and Getting Help

One piece of practical advice that became a theme when speaking to female entrepreneurs was, "Get help as soon as possible." It was clearly a lesson that most of these women wanted to pass on. As financial consultant Sandra Baptiste shared, "It would have cut the journey in half had I gotten help early on."

Why are women so hesitant to ask for help? Are we afraid to appear like we can't do it all? Are we afraid that we might come off looking unintelligent? Are we concerned that others can't do it as well as we could? Do you want to be portrayed as superheroes who can leap tall buildings in a single bound, run a successful business, manage a family and still come off looking calm and put together? Do you want to take all the credit for your work and stand like Wonder Woman with your hands on your hips declaring, "I did it all on my own." Or do you want to play the role of the overworked and overwhelmed, "having it all" power player like Sarah Jessica Parker's character in the movie, *I Don't Know How She Does It?* You may want to stop and ask yourself why you're avoiding asking others for help.

See if you identify with any of these common excuses:

- "I don't want to seem like a bother."
- "What will they think of me if I ask them for help?"
- "Who am I to ask them for help?"
- "It's too tough to explain to someone else what to do."
- "It'll take so much time to delegate these tasks. It's faster if I just did them myself."
- "Someone else might mess things up and I'll just have to fix it in the end."
- "It is just more trouble than it's worth."
- "It's just too large of an expense especially since I'm in the start-up phase and trying to bootstrap."
- "I'm secretly a control freak and can't stomach the thought of letting go of aspects of my business or delegating tasks."

Getting the necessary help in business is a necessity. It isn't a luxury or something nice to have down the road. If you are going to run a successful business, it's imperative you seek out the guidance, expertise, wisdom and assistance from others. You may be in business for yourself, but you don't have to do everything yourself. It's time to begin acting like the head of your company which means delegating task, hiring help and seeking the expertise and advice of others. The sooner, the better.

Find your advisors and mentors early on so you can turn to them when challenges arise. There will inevitably be highs and lows along your path, and when you find yourself bumping up against a wall, you won't have to retreat and then spiral down into a pity party. The key is to reach out to others who have ventured this path for advice and guidance. This advice can come in many different forms: a contact who can make an introduction to a potential customer lead, an expert in your field who has experience maneuvering the product development landscape, or a seasoned entrepreneur who would be open to sharing how they navigated a particular thorny issue in your industry.

Jenee Dana of Focus Opus isn't shy about asking questions or asking for connections. She actively reaches out to people and asks, "What's the next step?" She believes you can solve any business problem if you just ask.

For Amy Riley, founder of Shoop Consulting, her first big ask was one of the most nerve racking. She went to her old employer and asked to be considered for a consulting contract. "I was so nervous telling her and asking to be considered." But it definitely paid off. Her former employer has been one of her biggest clients to date and the relationship is still going strong.

Whatever the question or concern is, there is someone out there who has been faced with similar challenges – and survived. Most people are happy to share their wisdom. As writer Jeryl Brunner shared, "People do like to help other people. It's how you ask, though." So when you're ready to ask, make sure your respectful of their time, come prepared with a specific question, be courteous, send a thank you note and find a way to give back.

In many cases you may have to hire a coach or consultant to get you clear on your path of action. It is an investment and one you shouldn't take lightly. Patty Lennon shared her views on hiring coaches. A life design coach, Patty struggled during the first year she launched her company Mom Gets A Life. Patty had an illustrious fifteen-year career in banking at Citigroup and had mentors all along the way. Now on her own, she realized she needed help believing that she could do what she loved and make good money at it. After working tirelessly her first year in business she only cleared $2,000. That wasn't going to cut it. She was reluctant to hire a coach but the time had come to do so. "She made me raise my prices within two weeks of working together by four hundred percent. It was scary," Patty shared. "I wouldn't have had the courage to do it unless she was standing there telling me I could do it."

Patty believes that fear stops a lot of people from hiring the help they need. Coming from a banking background she still thinks like a banker, "People have a fear of the dollars involved. People need to understand every good investment has a return on that investment – the ROI. It's important if you own a business to think like a business person – like a CEO." She realized that if she wanted her business to grow and to continue growing she would need to make the investment and ask for help. It has paid off for Patty. Her business is thriving, she has been frequently written up in the press and she recently held the first of many Mom Gets A Business Conference this past year.

Asking for help isn't only about getting guidance and assistance for work-related matters. Getting help is also crucial in your personal life as well. Fortunately in this day and age, services are plentiful that can help make your life a bit easier, but often it's a matter of making some changes at home and asking others to pitch in.

Chalene Johnson, fitness expert and entrepreneur, noted in a conference I recently attended that her whole business turned around when she hired someone to come to her house three hours a day for just three days a week to do simple chores. Chalene, who works from her beautiful home office in Southern California, found that doing laundry was her procrastination tool. With an active family including a husband and two kids, it's easy for the laundry to pile up, and if she knew there was laundry to do she'd find herself in the laundry room. Even though it was an expense she didn't initially think she could afford, she quickly realized that by freeing up her time, she was able to work on more important things, like her business. It also freed her up to spend more time with her family when she wasn't working. The year she hired Inez was the year her business took off, from half a million in debt to having a profit of over a million that year.

Laundry came up again with Jennifer Adams Bunkers, founder of TruKid, a company focused on natural body care products for kids. She delegates everything that she can both professionally and personally. And, she simply doesn't do laundry. With six kids varying from high-school age on down, she has plenty of hands to help out. Everyone pitches in the Bunkers house. Socks in particular became a hot topic recently. You can imagine how difficult it must be to keep socks with their partners and in the drawers of the respective kids. Jennifer was advised by a fellow mother to keep a big basket where all the socks for every kid was tossed in. Then as someone is ready for a pair of socks they go in and fetch the ones they need. She was relieved to find a unique solution to a situation that would come up when you're managing a family of eight. Women everywhere have clever solutions to problems so ask others what they are doing to make life a little bit easier.

Challenge: Let's Play a Game – Delegate or Ditch

We all have aspects of our lives that we don't enjoy doing, require a lot of time for little benefit, or don't allow you to focus on what's most important.

What aspects of your business can you delegate, outsource, or just plain ditch?

What areas of your personal life can you delegate, hire for, or just plain ditch?

Often you think that you can't afford to outsource certain tasks, but you have to ask yourself, how can you afford not to?

If you're spending two hours a day doing chores rather than working on your business, what's that really costing you? Sit down and do the math. You'll be surprised what you will learn.

What areas of your life can you ask for help?

What aspects of your business or life can you simply ditch?

It is easy to sit in your office struggling away in isolation. You may fumble around trying different things and finding yourself bumping up against challenges, one after the other. The lonely path isn't the smart path – and it's definitely not the easy road. We are social creatures. We love connecting with real, live people and exchanging ideas, stories, advice, challenges, solutions and best practices. We thrive within healthy relationships – both the people we work with and those that we serve. We are energized by interactions and meaningful exchanges. This is true in life and this is especially true for business. Don't play Lone Wolf. Go out and meet people. Develop deep, lasting relationships. Get help and seek advice. Surround yourself with quality people, get the guidance you need, lead from a place of strength, confidence and passion and go after it!

Spotlight: Dina Proctor From Rock Bottom to Rocking It

There is something to be said about timing. As the end of 2008 drew near, Dina Proctor found herself at an emotional rock bottom. She was unhappy as an administrative assistant and privately she was dealing with alcohol addiction and food issues. She was on the verge of suicide and knew she desperately needed help.

She was able to pull herself out of her depression and is now helping others to do the same. "My biggest challenge was leaving behind the security of a corporate firm – not knowing where the next dollars would come from," Dina shared. This is a common concern that comes up but like so many other women she knew that she had to follow her path and had to trust that the money would come in to support her.

Her unique and quick method of mediation which she created and used in her recovery, as well as uses with her clients, has even caught the eye of Jack Canfield, Dr. Bruce Lipton and many others. Often the tools that someone uses to regain their life, are the tools and skills that many woman take into the world to help others. This is the case with Dina and she has created great business success with it as well.

Timing is everything and we're reminded of this with Dina. If she had devised her business even five or ten years earlier, it would have been a much tougher and slower route to gain visibility and success. Until recently, there wasn't the ability to market directly to customers like there is now through social media platforms such as Twitter, Facebook and Pinterest. Building, managing and updating high-quality websites is much cheaper and easier as well. We live in an amazing time and have access to technology and customers that would have only been a dream twenty years ago. Dina has also published a book which would have been a costly endeavor typically costing over ten thousand dollars (plus a garage full of books) only a few years ago. With self-publishing becoming more mainstream and print-on-demand a reality, there is no inventory to house and a nominal initial investment.

What Dina particularly loves about her business in today's reality is that she can travel and work anywhere she likes due to the advances and affordability of technology and other supportive tools. "The world is my office," she shared.

We truly live in a phenomenon time, where everyone has access (usually affordable) to tools and technologies that can grow a significant business. And if you need help, you can get it with a simple click of a mouse from people in every corner of the world. There is nothing that can stop you. The barriers to entry are disappearing with each passing year.

Inspiration Library

Music
With a Little Help From my Friends by The Beatles
Independent Woman by Destiny's Child
I'll Stand by You by The Pretenders
Umbrella by Rihanna
Call Me Maybe by Carly Rae Jepsen

Movies
Divine Secrets of the Ya-Ya Sisterhood
Steel Magnolias
Mona Lisa Smiles

Books
By Invitation Only: How We Built Gilt and Changed the Way Millions Shop by Alexis Maybank and Alexandra Wilkis Wilson
Tribes: We Need You to Lead Us by Seth Godin
Your Network Is Your Net Worth: Unlock the Hidden Power of Connections for Wealth, Success, and Happiness in the Digital Age by Porter Gale
Stiletto Network: Inside the Women's Power Circles That Are Changing the Face of Business by Pamela Ryckman
Make a Name for Yourself: Eight Steps Every Woman Needs to Create a Personal Brand Strategy for Success by Robin Fisher Roffer

CHAPTER 7

Get Energized

> "She was full of some strange energy that morning.
> Her every movement had purpose and life and she
> seemed to find satisfaction in every little thing."
> —Anna Godbersen, *Envy*

Business books hardly mention the role that energy plays on finding and maintaining success. As I spoke to successful female entrepreneurs, there was no shortage of energy as well as enthusiasm. It permeated through the phone lines and was wildly contagious. Often I got off the phone with these ladies and I felt like I just had a triple espresso. Their energy was boundless yet grounded and genuine. They were excited to reflect on their past challenges and how they overcame them, as well as share what motivates and drives them. They were thrilled to impart their advice and insight and to help other women find the courage to venture out on their own. Most loved exploring the idea why women entrepreneurial role models didn't come to mind when they started out in business. After every call I wondered *how do they maintain this level of energy day in and day out?*

With this question at the forefront of my mind, I started to dive deeper into their routines and ways that they kept themselves going at such prolonged high speeds. I expected to hear dirty little secrets such as: they consume pots of coffee each day, live solely on energy drinks like you so often hear about in technology start-ups, or they partake in Ritalin, diet stimulants or your standard elicit drugs. Nope. That wasn't the case.

Are these women just lucky? Were they born with boundless energy? Do they have access to a mysterious pill like Bradley Cooper consumed in the movie *Limitless*?

What successful women have is an uncanny way, often learned through experience and self-insight, to manage their energy in such a way that their activities generate even more energy. They are energized by their passions. They eliminate toxic activities that drain their precious resource. And, they find ways to cultivate and produce even more energy through physical exercise, healthy socializing and quieting their minds.

Being Overwhelmed is So Last Year

> "Many of us feel stress and get overwhelmed not
> because we're taking on too much, but because we're
> taking on too little of what really strengthens us."
> —Marcus Buckingham

For most women launching their own enterprise, they find themselves overwhelmed by not only the changes they are making to their personal life, but also by all the tasks they need to do to get their business up and running. I once heard someone compare business to launching the space shuttle. The majority of the energy and fuel used is during takeoff in order to get the nearly five-million ton shuttle off the ground. The same goes for business. Much of your energy is expended during the first few years to get your business off the ground. It can be exhausting but also immensely rewarding.

For years being overwhelmed, over-scheduled and over-worked has been worn like a badge of honor. I particularly saw this play out when I was in the corporate world and with my friends who are attorneys. It felt like it was a competition. The winner was always the one who looked like she hadn't slept in days and who complained most about how much work she has to do and how little free time she had for personal affairs. I'd hear of stimulant abuse and how women were purchasing diet drugs from across the border (knowing the U.S. had banned these substances because they led to serious heart problems and even death). The diet drugs played two roles: obviously the drugs kept weight off but more importantly they boosted energy. When I jumped ship from executive recruiting, I continued to foster a Type A personality during graduate school and into the early months of my own business. But what I quickly realized is that it no longer made sense – in fact, it never made sense. I had to consciously break myself of that bad habit. It didn't make me any more productive and, in actuality, it made me less efficient and increasingly dissatisfied, unhappy and unhealthy.

You can have a lot on your plate without having massive and unhealthy levels of overwhelm. There are three culprits that can lead you down the road to Overwhelm City:

- Time Wasters
- Time Thieves
- Time Machine

Before I launch into the three culprits, it's important that you are clear on what your overarching goals are and what's most important to you. It may be your big why, as we talked about in Chapter 4, your mission statement, or the completion of a particular project, program or product. When you have a clear purpose for your business or stage of your business, you can use that as a filter to sift all your existing tasks and activities through. As Heather Jackson of Heather Jackson Yoga of Calgary, Canada shared, "You have to be really clear on your why because so much can be overwhelming. But why moves you to action and creating." If you keep your mission in plain sight near your desk and computer, it can remind you what is of the utmost importance – and it isn't looking up your high school boyfriend on Facebook.

Time Wasters

Time Wasters are simply those activities that are a complete waste of your time. Everyone has them. We mistakenly think we're working, but what we're calling "work" in reality is definitely not moving our projects and passion forward. In fact, they're forms of distraction, procrastination and usually resistance to doing more important activities. Examples might be: non-focused and excess use of social media, checking and re-checking email, obsessively checking your analytics or other numbers, constantly monitoring your competition, or gossiping. This extends to your personal life, too. You might find that you belong to groups that you've outgrown or don't enjoy any longer. You may have joined them years ago and now feel obligated to attend. Check in with your personal calendar and see what you can let go of that is no longer enjoyable or necessary.

Time Thieves

Time Thieves are tasks and activities that are a necessary part of business but take up or steal a lot of your time. You may do them because you find them easy to do or you don't want to spend the money to pay someone else to do them. You may unconsciously or even consciously be afraid of loosening the reins of control. Examples may be: bookkeeping, social media, customer service, scheduling appointments, accounting, marketing and so on. In your personal life, it may be housekeeping, laundry, running errands or grocery shopping. These activities are stealing time away from the important work – the work that is in your Zone of Genius. Gay Hendricks writes about finding your Zone of Genius in his book, *The Big Leap*. He outlines how most people find themselves working in their Zone of Competence, performing activities and doing work that they're competent in, or in their Zone of Excellence, performing activities and tasks that they're excellent in executing and that they usually get praise and applause for. These two zones are comfortable and often easy but the tasks, behaviors and actions in these areas aren't pushing you towards your genius. In fact, you're stalling out here because you're afraid to step fully into your purposeful work – the place of your genius. This applies to not only the work we choose to do in general, but in our daily tasks as well.

According to Hendricks, there are four questions to ask yourself in order to make the leap into your Zone of Genius:

1. What do I most love to do?
2. What work do I do that doesn't seem like work?
3. In my work, what produces the highest ratio of abundance and satisfaction to amount of time spent?
4. What is my unique ability?

If you are designing a line of clothing, does it make sense to be spending a third of your time doing bookkeeping and shopping for retail space? Your genius most likely is in design and maybe in the leadership of your company, not on entering numbers into a spreadsheet. That is someone else's genius, so hire someone who is a genius with numbers.

In the category of time thieves, I also include toxic relationships. Are there people in your life that are sucking the wind out of your sails? Everyone, at one point or another, has had people in their life that are toxic. They're excessively negative or cynical. These are the people that, when you walk away from spending time with them, you feel drained and exhausted. Relationships don't need to feel like that. Even if a friend is going through a rough patch, you shouldn't feel like you've aged five years after having coffee with them. They may also demand an excessive amount of your time. You may need to evaluate the relationship and whether it's healthy for you to continue. You may decide that it's either time to cut the cord or phase the relationship out gradually and gracefully. By closing the door to these relationships, you will find energy reserves you didn't even know existed and you will make room for healthy and happy new relationships to enter as well.

Time Machine

I call the last culprit the Time Machine. This sneaky cause of overwhelm happens when your mind is not present in the here and now. You are either licking your wounds regarding past mistakes or you're constantly worried about what might go wrong in the future. This future-tripping can turn into a self-fulfilling prophecy if you're not careful. The fear of uncertainty of the future causes people to run through the gamut of "what ifs" and worse case scenarios. You may believe that you're being proactive in preparing yourself for the worst, but you're only attracting the worse case to find you. As Buddha reminds us: "All that we are is the result of what we have thought. The mind is everything. What we think we become."

In order to overcome your self-created feelings of overwhelm, you need to be firmly planted, both feet and your whole head in the present moment. Yes, I'm talking about mindfulness. It can be tough to be mindful at first, but with awareness and practice, you will find that it will blast away your overwhelm and open the door to success and happiness.

Remember that what you pay attention to – your thoughts, beliefs, inner dialogue – is your clearest predictor of your future.

Saying No

> "A 'No' uttered from the deepest conviction is better than a 'Yes' merely uttered to please, or worse, to avoid trouble."
>
> —Mahatma Gandhi

How comfortable are you with saying no? For many women it is one of the hardest things to do yet as an entrepreneur you need to learn how to – and fast. You may be afraid of losing clients or prospective business or looking less than generous with your time. In the early days you may find yourself saying yes to every request for coffee or networking opportunity in order to increase your visibility and connections. You may agree to speak at events, take on projects or respond at significant length to every request, including those probing about your business. Many books advise saying yes to every opportunity that comes your way because you don't want to miss that potential one golden opportunity. This is based in a scarcity mindset. The notion that there are only a few perfect opportunities available and once you miss them, that's it, they're gone. That just isn't true. You can be open to opportunities and thoughtfully accept ones that make sense and decline those that do not. Opportunities, connections, clients, customers are truly limitless if you believe that is the case. You have every right to be as selective as you want to be.

You may find this pattern of saying yes is seen in your personal life, too. If so, it's not a bad idea to start using no in this arena as well. How often do you agree to do things you later regret? Let's say someone asks you to proofread his lengthy and error-filled resume, a friend comes into town and wants to stay with you for two weeks, or you join a book club you had no intention of joining but just couldn't say no?

We all have a lot to do and many responsibilities on a daily and weekly basis. If you're not able to firmly decline activities and favors that people ask of you, you're heading down the boulevard of burnout. It's easy to allow this to happen, too. You have great intentions and you believe you're being helpful, compassionate and generous, but really you're spreading yourself increasingly thinner as your time and energy are pulled in a thousand different directions. Here are some strategies to get you started on the no express:

1. Instead of always saying yes when people ask something of you, take a moment and say, "Let me get back to you." It gives the person a tentative answer and gives you time to ponder whether the opportunity is worth your valuable time and energy.

2. Create a company policy, especially around areas where you're particularly vulnerable to saying yes. You may think this is premature when you're the sole person in your company or in the early years, but it will save you hours of wasted time now and in the future. It can be around coffee dates, taking on particular types of clients, accepting special requests, bartering arrangements or partnerships. Having a policy you refer to makes it much easier to say you're not interested.

3. Trust your instinct. If a request or opportunity just plain doesn't feel right, say no. Your gut is your strongest ally, so trust it. If you still are questioning the opportunity, seek out the counsel of a trusted business advisor. Often when you simply hear yourself explaining the situation out loud, you discover the answer was there all along.

4. If the same questions are asked of you frequently, include a FAQ on your website that you can direct people to.

Also, create templates that you or your staff can use in response to email or written requests that you can tweak as needed. This way you're not recreating the same responses time and again.

Successful entrepreneurs know the value of saying no and keeping firm with their boundaries. As they rise in their influence and reach, they become increasingly aware that they need to create firm boundaries in order to protect two of their most valuable resources: time and energy. For Christiane Lemieux, founder of modern furniture and home decor brand, Dwell Studio, saying no was a lesson she learned early on. "You need to learn to say no if something is pretty far off from your original vision. Women seem to be programmed to say yes a lot and it's hard to say no. But you need to put aside people-pleasing," said Christiane. She says she's getting better with saying no but it's something she still has to work on.

There is no greater time than now to create these boundaries and discover firm and creative ways to say no. Remember, when you say no to something, you are essentially saying yes to yourself and the grander vision you have for your company. So, what opportunities or areas of your life can you say a firm yet gracious no to?

Practicing Self Care

"Usually, when the distractions of daily life deplete our energy, the first thing we eliminate is the thing we need the most: quiet, reflective time. Time to dream, time to contemplate what's working and what's not, so that we can make changes for the better. (January 17)"

—Sarah Ban Breathnach, Simple Abundance:
A Daybook of Comfort and Joy

In addition to business books neglecting the topic of one's energy, they hardly speak about the importance of good self-care for entrepreneurs. They gloss over it as though the body is of no matter compared to the feverishly plotting mind. When you watch interviews of twenty-something technology startup folks, they take pride in their overnighters and the ability to survive on sugary energy drinks, caffeine and take-out. But the wear of sleep deprivation, lack of sunlight and improper nutrition is clearly seen on their skin. They look grey and weathered. Regardless, they wear it as a badge of honor as though it's the price of admission to declare themselves a "start-up founder." They may be able to get away with it for a few years, or maybe even a decade, but for most of us this isn't desirable, sustainable or in any way conducive to the life we envision. We want to start companies to contribute to the world and to design a life that includes family, friends, community, hobbies, activities and travel. We didn't quit our traditional jobs to create a new, self-made prison. We created a business in order to create freedom.

We've discussed heart-related matters in past chapters, especially around the topic of passion – that fiery heart-centered desire to chase after something with everything you've got.

But the physical heart, that blood-rich, vital organ that persistently beats without conscious permission, is one that you need to also keep firmly in mind.

What kills more women each year is not usually what people think. According to the National Institutes of Health (NIH), one in four women dies from heart disease in the United States. In fact, coronary heart disease —the most common type of heart disease—is the number one killer of both women and men in the U.S. It may seem dramatic to bring up heart disease when we're talking about building a business, but it's important if you're going to be a powerful, purposeful entrepreneur that you take care of your body and mind so that you can witness all the fruits of your labor as they unfold.

Heart disease is preventable and you can make significant changes now to ensure that you keep your ticker running strong for many many years to come.

If you ran a Fortune 100 company, your health would be monitored, and you'd be sent to places such as the Cleveland Clinic to run a battery of tests to ensure you're healthy. When you're running a multi-billion dollar company with stake holders, thousands of employees, millions of customers, and investors who have a vested interest in you, you better believe the health of the CEO is important. Similarly, you are the CEO of your company — and often its biggest shareholder. You need to take your health and wellness seriously as well.

It goes without saying that you need to get regular exercise. Exercise doesn't need to be relegated to a gym and group classes. You can move your body simply by taking a vigorous walk, dancing, chasing your active kids, practicing martial arts, taking a hike or roller skating. Find activities that you truly enjoy. It makes it much easier to stick to. You can even recruit a friend which helps you stick with it and gives you an opportunity to catch up regularly. Variety is truly the spice of life, so mix up your exercise routine: take in a new class, try a sport you'd never consider, join a team, or strap on a pair of roller blades. Have fun with it.

Jessica Herrin of Stella & Dot values the time away from her multi-million dollar company. "My best ideas come when I distance myself from day-to-day operations. It gives me a fresh perspective and energy," Jessica shared in an interview for *Savor the Success Magazine*. When she isn't stylishly running around her company, she is spending time with her family, running, or skiing. She finds that getting away from the business is also a great way of clearing her mind and inviting room for creativity.

So when you use the excuse that you're too busy to exercise because you have so much on your to do list, consider that exercise may be just the solution you need at the moment. Moving energy creates more energy. (And what entrepreneur doesn't want more energy)?

Even if you're all set with a great exercise routine and you're active on a regular basis, it may not be enough to manage stress. You also need to discover and foster other ways to cope with stress. As an acupuncturist, I see a ton of people who are super active yet they are horrible at managing their stress. They believe that exercise is all they need. It's a great start, and thankfully they have that outlet, but it often isn't nearly enough, especially during difficult times. You need to discover other techniques to manage the increasing stress that may arise as you start and grow your business. Here are just a few ideas, hardly exhaustive but a good place to start:

- Meditation
- Yoga
- Tapping/EFT
- Psychotherapy, hypnotherapy, counseling
- Acupuncture (couldn't resist adding this one)
- Talking with a supportive friend
- Couples therapy
- Massage and other forms of body work

Consider it vital for your business that you take care of your heart and your health. Most successful women have realized this and have incorporated wellness into their daily or weekly routine. And there is a beautiful benefit many find in doing so. Like Jessica Herrin noted, time away from the business helps stir creativity and promotes discovering solutions to problems.

Self care includes exercise, but there are so many different ways to take care of yourself, relax, and rejuvenate. Self care can take many different forms and is dependent on what you like. What you may consider self care may not appeal to someone else. But it is important to identify forms of self care that speak to you. To help you identify all the ways you can foster time for yourself and promote relaxation and rejuvenation, I've included a list below to get you thinking.

Spotlight: Heather Jackson On Caring for Herself and Others

Role models for women entrepreneurs can come in all shapes and sizes and be of any age. Heather was recommended to me by another entrepreneur, Jackie Dumaine who wrote me, "Although she is only 24 years old (24!), she is a spitfire and has achieved so much success in the few months that I've known her. She has a deep personal story that touches my heart, and her courage in overcoming adversity inspires me. I admire her with all of my heart." With that introduction, I just had to pick up the phone to speak with her. Heather radiates joy and compassion as soon as you meet her. Wise beyond her years, she shared how she has grown her business.

Not shy about using "entrepreneur" to describe herself, which of course I love, she shared with me how she is going through an exciting phase of "really putting myself out there and engaging." She is not only a yoga instructor, but has a Health Promotion degree. After working closely with oncologists and psychotherapists during her practicum with the Healing and Cancer Foundation in Canada, where she helped facilitate workshops to help people undergoing treatment for a cancer diagnosis, she had a vision of bringing all the elements of her education and training together. As she shared, "I wondered how can I make this into a business and really be of service and step into this fully." She confessed that it was easy to get overwhelmed by overwhelm and other self-limiting beliefs such as, "I'm too young" and, "How am I going to do all of this?" She overcame these thoughts by becoming very clear on her why. "My why is more so my purpose. I felt so strongly about this, it's my internal drive. It's checking back in with this when things get chaotic." She also shared how she maintains her energy level when there is always so much to do.

"Things are constantly changing, demands are placed on you," she shared, "You have to ask yourself, 'Am I being congruent with the work I'm doing?'" For Heather, who supports other individuals on their therapeutic journey, it's important that she is clear and healthy herself. To keep herself grounded, she has daily rituals that she sets as reminders to slow down and take time to breathe. As expected for a yoga instructor, her yoga practice is core to making sure she stays healthy. However, she doesn't put unrealistic demands on herself. "I make sure I do yoga every day, even it's ten minutes to sit and do a bit of practice. It helps me be more grounded and more congruent with what I do."

Challenge: Rev Up Your R&R

Stress can zap you of energy and will likely create unhealthy habits and unhappiness. We can't have that. Here are some examples of ways to relax and recharge:

- Get some perspective. It is easy to spend every waking moment thinking about your business. Take a weekend or an afternoon off. Find other activities to give your mind a temporary vacation.
- Take a yoga class.
- Go dancing with friends. Or, have a dance party at home.
- Mix up your physical activities. If you always go running, try a spin class instead. If you can't imagine not going for a run, then take a different route or do interval work.
- Go to a museum, gallery or an exhibit.
- Do some volunteer work. There is nothing more satisfying than helping others out.
- Take in a group cooking class.

- Schedule a date with a girlfriend, or better yet, schedule a mini vacation.
- Meditate. Many active women are resistant to mediation, but you can easily find ten minutes a day to sit quietly and turn off the faucet of running thoughts. There are plenty of guided mediations available if you prefer that method as well.
- Play your favorite song or create a playlist for those times when you want to relax (or get energized).
- Get outside and take in some fresh air. There is nothing like taking a walk in nature to quiet the mind.
- Take a bath with calming essential oils such as lavender. Light some candles and soak in the bliss.
- Read a non-business related book.
- Go to a movie. It's so easy to get distracted at home watching a movie, but when you're in dark theater where it would be rude to turn on your blinding phone, you are able to better get lost in the story.
- Buy some fresh flowers.
- Prepare a beautiful meal from all new recipes.
- Go to an amusement park and act like you're fifteen years old again.
- Make a date with your significant other and promise not to talk about work, kids or money.
- See a live show — music, performance art, comedy, musical, theater. Whatever strikes your fancy.
- Plan your next vacation.
- Spend a day shopping or window-shopping, alone or with a friend.
- Turn off your phone, computer and all other noisy devices for one whole day.
- Try scrapbooking, vision boarding, drawing, painting or another visually artistic endeavor.
- Revive or discover your green thumb by an afternoon of gardening.
- Explore a new town or simply a new part of your town.
- Perform a totally random act of kindness (and don't tell anyone about it).

Your turn! Let's create a long, exhaustive list of everything that rejuvenates and relaxes you. Nothing is too simple or too luxurious. Be as creative and outrageous as possible.

Include simple luxuries such as taking in a new yoga class or soaking in a hot bath or, perhaps, drinking a cappuccino while reading a book at a cafe.

But also include some more opulent choices such as: a day of pampering at your local spa, a family get-away to the lake or a summer in the South of France learning to cook.

Most of all, have fun creating this list. Schedule time, like you would an appointment, for self care. Some of the larger items could be set on your calendar as celebratory rewards for hitting certain milestones.

Remember, self care is not a luxury. It is necessary for health and happiness and just makes good business sense.

The Myth of Balance

> "There is no such thing as work-life balance. Everything worth fighting for unbalances your life."
> —Alain de Botton

We have been sold an idea that balance is possible, and we have found ourselves struggling to discover the secrets that others have seemingly perfected. From the outside, they seem to have it all: the perfect business or career, the harmonious family, the time to send cookies off to school for bake sales, the sculpted arms, tidy house and the energy to maintain it all. It's the picture of perfection — and the legend of fiction.

Thanks to our foremothers in the Feminist Movement who fought for equal rights and the ability to do and have it all, we have been given the choices and freedoms we often take for granted today. It wasn't all that long ago that we weren't even able to vote in the United States (although let's face it, we still haven't seen a female president yet). These strong trailblazing women opened doors for us and told us that we could have it all. Through the years, we've embraced that *have it all* attitude thinking we can have it all right now – all of it at the same time. In doing so, we have put an enormous amount of pressure to have the ideal career or business, have a family, participate in various social and community activities, keep physically and spiritually fit and somehow do it all with grace and ease. We seek out the elusive balance that everyone keeps talking about only to discover that it's impossible to find, let alone maintain. The worst part, when you aren't feeling balanced by these impossible standards, you feel guilty or worse — you feel like a failure. The balance we hear so much about is a myth. Found to be even more elusive as a blossoming entrepreneur. Stop chasing this mythical creature. Give yourself a break. Find another way.

It's easy to fall prey to the myth. I surely did. As this project progressed through the months, I began to wonder how these women were managing family and business. From the outside, they appeared to have it all, especially the booming business and the growing family – two things I desperately wanted. At home, I was finding it increasingly difficult balancing all my roles, and I felt like my projects, business, health and personal life were all taking a significant hit. I thought someone must have the secret or at least have a few clever ideas that I was missing. I began to ask the women I was interviewing how they did it, hoping someone – anyone – had the magical answer to this modern dilemma. What I found, however, is that everyone seeks balance, thinks about it frequently and considers the alternatives. And yet, in the end, no one has the answer.

Like my own search, many women believe an answer exists but that they haven't been so lucky to figure it out, either. It's the 21st Century equivalent of the Loch Ness Monster: We think it may be real, there have been the occasional sightings, yet we have no real proof that it actually exists. What this tells us is that there may not actually be one answer to this common problem inflicting the modern woman.

The myth is born out of a few false beliefs. One belief that I have been fiercely holding onto and slow to dissolve, is that everyone else has discovered the secret and I'm clueless. We're all guilty of looking at other people and assuming they have it all figured out. We see their public persona and pictures that grace the covers of magazines or their Facebook profiles and imagine that everything is rosy and perfect. We envy how they appear to have a healthy happy family and a booming business. We don't actually know what areas they may be neglecting, if any, or what sacrifices they've made. Maybe they've had their ups and downs and have learned valuable lessons in the process, and, like everyone, is figuring it out as they go.

Another aspect of this myth is that we blame being out of balance for the cause of our fatigue, restlessness and lack of energy. We assume that if we are spending equal time in all areas of our life then our energy levels should be off the hook. But we all know that it isn't the amount of time we spend in our various activities, but it's the quality of time spent that matters. For example, your work can be exhilarating and create boundless energy while your personal life might be draining and exhausting. When it comes to your own business, you may find your work fuels you in new and inspiring ways and you absolutely love what you're doing. When it comes to balancing or integrating the different aspects of our lives, it's important to take a closer look at priorities and what's most important to you and what's working well. After a careful look, you may find you need to make some adjustments.

Many of the women I spoke to recognize that they're out of balance in their life, but they wouldn't have it any other way – at least right now.

It's not so much about finding a balance per se, but in finding where your values and priorities lie and what generates energy for you.

From the outside, Mia Bauer, founder of Crumbs Bake Shop, looks to have found balance. She founded a successful cupcake retail empire which started in her Upper Westside neighborhood in New York City, is a mother of two darling kids, works alongside her husband, and vacations in the Hamptons. I thought she may have the secret I was searching for. Mia was honest when I asked her how she balances family and work. "I feel guilty about this answer, but in reality, I spent as much time as possible with the business and with my family. I rarely slept and worked all night. But there is a silver lining. I was really happy doing it. I didn't feel like I had no choice. I felt fulfilled." She shared that sacrificing sleep was well worth it to be able to grow a multi-million dollar brand while raising two young kids. Mia absolutely loved growing her business, yet didn't miss out on spending quality time with her family. I further wondered if she was one of those lucky women who has boundless energy. She laughed when I asked her this and said she definitely is not, but interestingly, has been perceived that way the last ten years. She attributes her energy to always wanting to achieve great things, her hard-working work ethic, and especially becoming a parent. The increase in her energy, this "new phenomenon," as she calls it, she treats as a gift. This gift surely has paid off. Mia successfully took the company public in 2011 and exited the following year. Due to a non-compete, this year has been about consulting for other burgeoning retail businesses, but the itch to start another business is back. Although when she left Crumbs she didn't think she'd start another retail food business because of the long hours and hard work, but she is considering taking the challenge on – again. I can't wait to see what Mia has up her sleeve next.

The areas where you are most passionate often get the most attention, but isn't that where you want to spend your time anyway?

Many women I interviewed agreed that usually something has to give in this equation, but it isn't for the long-term, and it isn't usually something that is of highest importance to them.

For Elizabeth Dehn of Beauty Bets and One Love Organics she admitted, "I'm not striving for balance. I'm striving to be happy and energized by life. To me balance looks like a lot of organized chaos." She shared that she, too, does not get enough sleep and goes hard then crashes. She knows that something is going to give and for Elizabeth it's her house. "My house is a mess most the time—and I've learned to be okay with that," she shared, which is no surprise given her hectic schedule running her beauty empire.

It didn't surprise me that Anne McCabe Triana, co-founder of CAM Private Wealth Services, shared that she views her life as a pie chart. "I'm constantly looking at the important silos: family, business, friends, health, and spirituality, and assessing where I am at that week or month." She admits that she isn't striving to have all the pieces of the pie balanced and equal. She believes that trying to juggle all areas of your life, which is nearly impossible to do, often leaves women feeling guilty. As the mother of a toddler, she shared, "It's important to be aware and self-assess, not in a negative way, but this enables you do something with the information." Like many women, she believes that women can have it all, just not necessarily at the same time. Her mindfulness to the different aspects of her life and prioritizing what's most important creates her own peace of mind.

Inevitably there will be times when aspects of your life will require more attention, time and energy. For instance, your child is sick and you have to take several days off to nurse him back to his rambunctious self. Other times, you're engrossed in a massive product launch and you're working late hours for a few weeks and missing social gatherings you had hoped to attend. Look, things come up. There is no way you can look at twenty-four hours in a day and equally portion a set number of hours to each area of your life. But when you look at the whole of your week, month or year, like Anne does, you may determine the areas that are the most important to you and allocate more time and energy to your highest priorities and make other adjustments as needed.

So is there an answer? Does the elusive secret exist (but is only known by a few select women)? I don't believe so. I believe you can surely learn many helpful tips and tactics from other women, but in the end, you need to figure out what works best for you. You need to look at your life and determine your utmost priorities. It really all comes down to what you value and your priorities. Once clearly articulated, it is your job to guard them closely and find ways to integrate other aspects when feasible. We're all in this together so when you do find solutions and tricks, share them with your sisters and help others out. It is challenging for all of us but we don't have to blindly figure this out on our own. Share what works and be open to receiving advice.

Spotlight: Chrisanna Northrup
On Finding Normal

Chrisanna Northrup is one busy lady. Her full time job is shrouding in mystery as a private banker for people who have a minimum of $10M in assets (most have over $500M). Being surrounded by accomplished, often self-made business people, she has realized that anyone can create gobs of success and abundance if they have the right attitude. She believes that there are no barriers to anything if you have a good business model and a good idea or concept. You can make it work. Looking to explore her creative side, she was inspired to write a movie script after having an incident with her children's nanny. Her "can do" and "anything's possible" attitude went to work and she picked up a book on how to write a screenplay. Before she knew it she had her script written and was ready to pitch. Figuring she had one shot to make this happen, Chrisanna decided that she would put a one-line ad in the Hollywood Reporter the day after the Oscars to see if she could land a deal. She had several calls and sold the screenplay for over six figures that very same week.

This was a huge turning point for Chrisanna – her creativity soared but her relationship with her husband plummeted. She was receiving a ton of media attention and was traveling around the country speaking about the project. When her interview with Rachel Ray aired, instead of celebrating such a successful moment she remembers crying over her failing marriage. She had three kids at home all under the age of eight years old and was a significant financial contributor to the household. Her kids and husband needed her and so she decided to turn off her creative outlets and focus on her family.

Five years went by and she was miserable. Her relationship was strained because she simply continued to ignored the fact that it wasn't working. She decided to move out and lived in an apartment while she and her husband worked on the relationship and she reengaged her creative side. The question of what makes couples extremely happy continued to haunt her and that fueled her next creative endeavor. "I was looking for answers. Who was doing it right? What can I learn from other people? I began to question whether these people existed," Chrisanna wondered.

Her curiosity on what made people extremely happy in relationships led her to conduct the largest study ever on relationships interviewing over 70,000 individuals from around the world. She brought in two leaders in their respective fields, relationship expert Dr. Pepper Schwartz and social science researcher Dr. James Witte, to co-author the project and book, *The Normal Bar: The Surprising Secrets of Happy Couples and What They Reveal About Creating a New Normal in Your Relationship*. It was a runaway success.

In an effort to improve her own relationship and using the knowledge she learned from the research, she and her husband periodically asked one another "What are the top 5 things we need from one another?" This simple question and the answers given have had a significant and positive impact on their lives. Nineteen years into their relationship, they are more in love now and happier than ever.

On Family

For many of the women I spoke with, their families continually motivate them and help define their ultimate success. Their families are a huge priority, and they are clear about that. When possible, they involve them in the business as well.

Jackie Dumaine, founder of The Yoga Code, had an awakening moment that took her life in a totally different direction. Four years ago, she found herself sitting alone in her car, paralyzed with fear and anxiety and deeply contemplating her life. She was your typical burnt-out executive and was desperately craving something new. Fortuitously, a yoga studio had opened up in her neighborhood and she decided her Type-A personality could use some adjustment. She fell in love with it and, in 2010, she left her six-figure job in advertising and traveled to an ashram in India to study yoga and meditation. Upon her return to Canada, she co-founded Stillness Room, a meditation furniture company which she recently sold, and then subsequently launched The Yoga Code. When I asked her what motivated her, she answered, "my family." She revealed that she has a 21 year-old son (which you would never guess when you look at her). She includes her family as much as possible in her business. "My mom comes to all my retreats. She is an integral part of creating community with retreat participants. It allows her to understand the nature of "what I do" and gives us time to bond," Jackie shared.

Farhana Dhalla took one of the most painful experiences a woman can go through and created a business and book out of it. On Valentine's Day, she discovered that her husband of ten years was cheating on her. She was in denial, hurt, and — at some level — relieved. They had three kids together, and Farhana wanted to go through the process of divorce as gracefully as possible. She took this painful situation and turned it into an opportunity for personal transformation and growth. She now guides others through the process of divorce and teaches them that this is a opportunity for self-reflection and personal development. One of her favorite aspects of being an entrepreneur, beside helping others during difficult times, is that her business has enabled her to be present for her three kids and participate in all their activities. She wouldn't have the opportunity to be so involved in a traditional job.

Amanda Johnson, author and founder of True to Intention, believes her ten-year-old son is a wise, old soul. When she comes up with new marketing ideas, she runs them past him. When she gets particularly excited about an idea her son will note, "Here's my mom running across the room in her underpants again." He definitely knows when his mom feels inspired. Amanda admitted, "Sometimes I'm totally out of balance but totally in alignment. I tell my family when I see the imbalance coming, and I not only ask them for support through it, I ask them what they need from me in the middle of it to stay happy." By including her family and getting them prepared for times when she is engrossed in a project, Amanda helps them feel involved and they're happy that she is doing what she loves.

Christina Daves realized she needed to reinvent herself at the age of forty-five years old. She has been working hard ever since she was fourteen years old and has had three distinct businesses before launching her most recent venture, CastMedic Designs, which provides stylish boots for women who have a foot or ankle injury. Diana Ross has even been spotted in one of her designs. Even with all the personal success, Christina had a turning point a few years ago when her teenaged daughter asked her, "Mom, when will we ever be able to make Christmas cookies together?" She knew that the retail store she was running at the time was all-consuming and she was missing out on important bonding activities with her kids. With her latest venture, she has created a business that allows her to spend much more time with her two kids. "I feel like I work all the time, but I'm able to still be a mom and I can do everything I want with my kids," she shared, even though she knows that might mean extended hours. She noted, "The downside is that it's no fun working at 11:00 at night if I wasn't able to finish what I was working on during the day." But for Christina, she wouldn't have it any other way.

Sandra Baptiste's main motivation is her son. Sandra was an accountant for over twenty years and lived both oversees and in the U.S. Ten years ago she had a calling to start her own business even though she was recently hired for a plum role within a company she was consulting for. When her son was born in 2004, she knew that her traditional job wasn't conducive to being a single mom, so she left and started her own firm working with CEOs, business owners and entrepreneurs. Sandra gleefully noted, "I'm motivated to be the best mom. I'm trying to show him you can live any life you want and that there is a different way of being." She believes that by living her best life she can inspire and influence her son to also live his best life as well.

Gemma Stone has a twinkle in her eye that draws you instantly in. Trained as a traditional psychologist, she found that her profession didn't speak to her heart. It has been a lesson in finding herself and her voice. "I've been in business seven years. The first three years I stayed in the box. The next two years I tiptoed out of the box. And finally the last two years, this is me – one hundred percent me," she shared. As she discovered her ideal business over time, she also has discovered what makes her most happy. Previously she was working all the time, her whole life consumed by her business. Now, every morning she has breakfast with her kids and family dinners every night. She is also able to have tea with her friends every Wednesday which is very important to her. She has created a business and life that also allows her husband to stay home with the kids. She is mindful of the challenges that come up as a mom running a business. She does a daily check to ascertain whether she is overbooked and if she is doing enough self-care because, as Gemma noted, "It's very easy to get consumed with business."

Jennifer Zeszut, CEO of Beckon, is one incredibly energetic person. When you get her on the phone, you know you're in for a ride. Her enthusiasm for her work comes through instantly and you can't help getting swept up in the excitement of her company and life. I was shocked to learn that she is also the mother of three children. There is a famous story she often shares that she specifically asked for a room with a strong WiFi connection during the birth of her third child because she was finalizing the sale of her first company. I guess when you're on your third kid, you know how certain things will transpire, so she was open to finalizing a bit of business before the baby arrived. She sold her company, Scout Labs, for $22.5 million the same day her son was born. When she came home with the new baby and told her two young kids, "Mom is not a CEO anymore," they sobbed. When she asked why they were so upset, they expressed that they know how being a CEO makes her happy and that she is so good at it. Jennifer clearly shares how much she loves her work with her kids and exposes them as much as possible to her business and leadership style. "Not every person in the world gets paid for what they love. My kids know that mom gets to do what she loves doing." She admits that she may not be able to attend every event but tries to include her kids, when she can, into some of her business activities. The week we spoke she took one of children to the florist to help pick out flowers for one of her employees. When I asked how she does so much, she, too, admits that she doesn't require much sleep.

So what does a woman who loves getting sleep to do? Can she be successful as well? For us sleeping beauties, we just have to be ruthless with our waking hours, know what we value most, say no and mean it, find meaningful ways to recharge and utilize our energy to the fullest. Remember, you can have whatever you want. You just have to be creative in finding a way to manage your passions and priorities while weaving together all the meaningful aspects of your life into one beautiful quilted masterpiece.

Spotlight: Kathy Korman Frey
– One Hot Momma

Kathy Korman Frey is one of those women you meet and you know she is a genuine champion for women. She is the creator of the Hot Mommas Project which is an award-winning social venture and the world's largest digital case study library of female role models. She had the idea for the project in 1998 and launched her first case study a few years later while teaching at the George Washington University School of Business, Center for Entrepreneurial Excellence. The stories include women from all walks of life, from princesses to CEOs, stay-at-home moms to students and everything in between. These teachable stories are rich, compelling and inspiring.

Kathy started her first company after her husband, an entrepreneur himself, noted that everyone was asking her for business advice. She wasn't sure if she was ready to give up "the pats on the head" to run her own venture. She knew she wanted to start a family, so decided to take a "swan dive into the unknown." The consulting firm she created was comprised of highly skilled part-time consultants who were some of the original "Hot Mommas." When people became more interested in the Hot Mommas Project over the consulting work, she realized she was onto something. Besides currently writing a book and her social and philanthropic activities, Kathy teaches her award-winning course, Women's Entrepreneurial Leadership at the George Washington University School of Business. "I'm motivated by making an impact – not just a difference, but an exponential impact," Kathy shared.

Although highly accomplished, she's a family gal. "I'm very close with my family and I want an active role in the lives of my kids. My definition of goals and motivation had to flex and expand to include this value, plus my business interests."

For Kathy, it's important to be happy and balanced in her life. "I seek out a type of equilibrium. If I don't have it, it's hard for me to rest until I either get it back or establish a new normal." I'm sure as a response to the modern issue of work-life balance, she's currently researching innovative part-time work models.

Inspiration Library

Songs
Let's Get Physical by Olivia Newton John
New Shoes by Paolo Nutini
Whatever songs energize, inspire or rejuvenate you.

Movies
Baby Boom
The Women (2008)

Books
The Big Leap: Conquer Your Hidden Fear and Take Life to the Next Level by Gay Hendricks, PhD
Peace Is Every Step: The Path of Mindfulness in Everyday Life by Thich Nhat Hahn
The Book of Secrets: Unlocking the Hidden Dimensions of Your Life by Deepak Chopra
The Magic of Thinking Big by Dr. David Schwartz
The Big Enough Company: Creating a Business That Works for You by Adelaide Lancaster and Amy Abrams

PART THREE:
Stepping Up Now
That You've Arrived

How your success will change your
life and the lives of others.

CHAPTER 8

What To Do When You've Arrived...
And Long Before

> 'But I don't want to go among mad people,' Alice
> remarked.
> 'Oh, you can't help that,' said the Cat: 'we're all
> mad here. I'm mad. You're mad.'
> 'How do you know I'm mad?' said Alice.
> 'You must be,' said the Cat, 'or you wouldn't have
> come here.'
>
> —Lewis Carrol, Alice's
> Adventures in Wonderland

#1 Secret Revealed

While interviewing over one hundred inspiring and successful women, I discovered the common threads that ran through each of these amazing women and witnessed glimpses of their uniqueness. Through our conversations, they articulated what it means to be an entrepreneur and what motivates them. They described their definitions of success and how they integrate family and business. They shared their challenges and how they overcame them. However, with each interview I became more intrigued with what wasn't spoken — those subtle qualities that took these women from brilliant ideas to brilliant implementors of those ideas. What became clear is a core aspect of why they've become successful — something that was illuminated by each and every woman. Some may have touched on it in a passing comment, but you could almost feel that with these women, there is something different about them.

The characteristic that they all had in common is also the primary secret to their success: a deep knowingness that they had to journey this entrepreneurial path, and that this path would ultimately lead to success. It is an understanding that speaks to them at a subtle yet deep gut level. They may not be entirely clear on how this knowingness will present itself in the world, but they're crystal clear that it's their job to find out. Words often cannot describe this drive other than they *just know*. And clearly it cannot be ignored. It is calling. It is an understanding. And it's truly a gift.

Some people may call this a gut reaction, instinct or intuition, but whatever label is used, they listen to the call. These role models also have learned to trust these internal cues and know that when they listen to them, they do not steer them wrong. Women naturally have an uncanny ability to listen and pick up the invisible signs that can help guide them. And this skill proves invaluable in business. This isn't just one person's opinion; it is, in fact, grounded in biology and physiology. Research has shown that the area of the brain that tracks gut feelings is actually larger and more sensitive in the female brain in comparison to the male brain. Gut feelings are not just free-floating emotions they are actual physical sensations that provide valuable information. Evolutionary biologists speculate that this ability to read emotional nuances gave our ancestors important cues for potential danger and the keen ability to protect their children.

Your gut is your biggest ally. Successful women have tuned into their intuition and that gut instinct to help guide them along their path. This internal navigation system is a gift, so listen to its guidance and use the information to propel you forward towards your dreams.

We're In Our Own Way – Again!

> "The fundamental cause of the trouble is that in
> the modern world the stupid are cocksure while
> the intelligent are full of doubt."
> —Bertrand Russell

There is a crazy phenomenon that arises in successful women. So, beware. It's so utterly absurd that women fall prey to this and nearly everyone at some point in their lives have felt this way. From Oprah Winfrey to Sheryl Sandberg, from Supreme Court judges to award-winning playwrights, from surgeons to superstars, there are very few accomplished women who seem to escape this.

In her book *The Secret Thoughts of Successful Women*, Valerie Young Ed.D. refers to this epidemic as the "impostor syndrome." Through her extensive research, she has found that highly accomplished and competent people often suffer from self-doubt. They're afraid of being found out, that someone will walk in and tell them they don't belong here, or that their success was a mistake. You may be seen as highly competent by the outside world, but you feel like you're just sliding by. As Dr. Young describes: "The impostor syndrome refers to people who have a persistent belief in their lack of intelligence, skills or competence. They are convinced that other people's praise and recognition of their accomplishments is undeserved, chalking up their achievements to chance, charm, connections and other external factors."

According to research conducted by psychologist Gail Matthews, seventy percent of people have impostor feelings at some point in their life. So you're clearly not alone. Not surprising, this is typically seen more often in women than men. Men do seem to experience this as well, but are better able to ignore it and move on.

Even when women have found success, their inability to internalize it in a healthy manner makes it further difficult for women to replicate it in the future. As Dr. Young noted, "they continually doubt their ability to repeat past successes. When they do succeed they feel relief rather than joy."

Does this sound familiar to you? Do you play down your successes? Do you secretly wonder if you really belong here? Do you wonder if you've gotten too big for your britches and you'll be eventually found out? Do you feel like you're just pretending, or worse – are a fraud?

There are many cultural reason why women often feel like frauds, including: the absence of praise as a child, our overly competitive education system, organizational cultures that feed on self-doubt, working in a creative field, working in a foreign country, or working alone. Although many if not all of these factors may play a role in your life, for our purposes, let's focus on how working alone can lead to feelings of being a fraud. Working alone is highly isolating and you can go days or even months without sharing your work or bouncing ideas off of another person. It's easy to begin second-guessing yourself when the only person on your team is you. Self-doubt creeps in and you may find yourself paralyzed to move forward. In order to prevent this from happening, it is critical, as mentioned in previous chapters, to seek out support from others, to find accountability partners who you can discuss your business with, and to connect with mentors and advisors who can provide sound guidance.

If you think that feeling like an impostor is something that you can secretly ignore and that it won't impact your business, think again. When you feel like an impostor, you have a greater tendency to undervalue yourself and your work. When you don't value your work, others tend not to value it, either. They won't take you seriously, they may believe your rates are inappropriate, or they will avoid doing business with you altogether.

When starting out in unknown territory like launching a business, it is easy to feel like you're playing a role and are not really a business person or entrepreneur. You may have all the credentials, experience, expertise and skills to prove otherwise, but that nagging feeling may still persist. And, it may persist many years into your business. It's important to know that you do belong here. Self-doubt, in small doses, is natural, but you need to tame the mental beast in your head that runs rampant stomping all over your self-worth. Review the factors that lead to feelings of impostor syndrome and ask yourself where your self-doubts historically came from. Work through teasing apart where you are now and how your accomplishments in the past came to fruition. Were they due to luck, chance, connections or charm? Or were they do to hard-work and diligence? Do you feel like you deserved your success? Do you feel like you deserve success in the future? Additionally, reflect on how you manage your impostor anxiety and how you keep from being found out.

You are a work-in-progress and learning as you go, but so is every other entrepreneur ahead of you on this journey. You will continue to gain more confidence and more insight as you become more competent and through experience. You just need to find productive ways to quiet the inner critic telling you that you don't belong and embrace the inner cheerleader who is thrilled you're here.

Toot Your Own Horn

> "So whatever you want to do, just do it... Making a damn fool of yourself is absolutely essential."
> —Gloria Steinem

One reason that came up over and again when I asked why women entrepreneurs are not in the media spotlight as much as they could be is that we're awful at tooting our own horns. We pride ourselves on humility and we believe it is frowned upon to gloat about one's accomplishments. You think Steve Jobs or Richard Branson had a difficult time sharing their wins or declined when a PR opportunity arose? I don't think so. It seems to be perfectly acceptable for men to brag, but for women it's considered unseemly.

As psychologist Carol Gilligan proposed in her book *In A Different Voice*, women have an innate drive to want to belong and an "obligation to exercise care and avoid hurt." We fear isolation and crave connection and community. We may unconsciously believe that our success and voicing our achievements may come with devastating consequences, including social isolation, loss of connection with family and friends, and perhaps being perceived less desirable by the opposite sex.

So how do you reconcile holding the female ethos of care, concern and connection with building a successful business and sharing your accomplishments? It may involve actually using these characteristics in a way you hadn't thought of before – through authenticity, vulnerability and storytelling.

As Peggy Klaus in her book, *Brag! The Art of Tooting Your Own Horn Without Blowing It*, notes:

> "Learning to brag is *not* about becoming something you aren't or trying to put something over on someone. In fact, bragging as an art is just the opposite. It's about becoming more of who you are and bringing forward your best parts with authenticity, pride, and enthusiasm. It's about telling your story in a way that showcases your strengths."

We have a false notion that if we put our heads down and work hard, the work will speak for itself or others will speak up on our behalf. It doesn't work that way, and men have a leg up knowing this. They have long understood the need for promoting oneself and aren't afraid of a little self-promotion. You need to realize that the best promoter of your work is you. You must find the strength and courage to speak up and share what you have to offer. You don't need to walk around wearing a neon sign advertising how awesome you are – unless that makes sense for you – but you can find authentic ways to share your work and your accomplishments. Storytelling and revealing aspects of your vulnerability as well as how you've overcome challenges are amazingly effective at illustrating your greatest strengths and achievements. Everyone loves a good story. You are, first and foremost, responsible for your own good press. You may be afraid that by sharing your wins you will make others feel less, but your achievements will only better your business and inspire those around you. You must ask yourself: If you're not sharing your story, who will?

Along with sharing your own stories and successes, sharing the wins and achievements of others not only promotes good karma but is good practice for your business too. It's important that we celebrate and share the successes of other business women. It's a good way to practice your brag muscle if you are a bit uneasy in the beginning bragging about yourself. Don't stay too long in your warm-up gear though. You do need to step out into the spotlight yourself and begin to brag about your achievements and wins as soon as possible.

In fact, speaking on behalf of others is much easier for women to do. Research has shown that women can negotiate on behalf of someone else more effectively than they do on their own behalf. Interestingly, they negotiate better than men do when both groups are asked to negotiate on the behalf of someone else. It's not all that surprising. Have you ever been to a cocktail party and a close friend gives you a glowing introduction? You may have looked around wondering who she was speaking about. Women are great at doing this. So when you have the opportunity to promote others' work, do so. It will come back in ways you'd never imagine.

Besides promoting our businesses and projects, it is our job, each and every one of us, to find ways to share our successes and strategies as well as our challenges with others who are sharing this path of entrepreneurism. Even if you're only two years in, you have substantial knowledge you can share with someone who is just starting out. However, she will never even know you exist unless you make yourself known. It is a duty to yourself as well as to girls and women everywhere to stand up and shine.

To be role models and examples to other women, we need to make ourselves known and step firmly into the spotlight. This is often the tricky part for most women. I'm not saying you have to live on an airplane doing the media circuit and morning television shows, but you can begin speaking up at community events or doing interviews for local papers. These are equally as important. Sign yourself or your business up to be considered for various media "Best Of" lists. Be open to speaking at events and sharing your story. There are hundreds of ways to promote your business and yourself. You just need to find the ones that you feel most comfortable with and even a few that push you outside your comfort zone. Remember: It's a fine line you need to learn to walk when it comes to listening to your gut and intuition and stepping outside what is cozy and comfortable. Check in with your internal navigation and decide if you're working from a place of fear or if your gut is giving you a legitimate warning. But keep in mind often just outside your comfort zone is where the magic happens.

Sometimes stepping into the spotlight means arousing some old fears, especially fear of public speaking. Public speaking is not a natural gift that some people were simply born with. It is a teachable skill, one where you often have to get out of your own way, and an invaluable one at that. People want to hear from you and about you. Women are yearning for authentic stories from those who've made it – or who have recently made the leap. Value that you have something important to share and then get out there and share it. There are wonderful training programs out there that help women find their voice and speak from a place of authenticity.

Great speaking isn't about being stiff and overly rehearsed. In her book *Transformational Speaking*, Gail Larsen shares how the best speakers "celebrate who they are and bring the essence of their true selves forward." People respond to speakers who are unapologetically real. Discover your signature story and speak from your heart. It will take you far.

Journeying Together

We have taken quite a journey together: from understanding the value and importance of role models to the depths of our mindset and motivation. You have discovered that what ultimately drives you can only be uniquely defined by you. You have learned the key behaviors that will get you started and keep you going as your company grows and expands. You have rediscovered the importance of your tribe and community and how to safeguard your energy to get the most out of each day.

Launching and growing a business can and will transform you. You will learn more about yourself and be challenged in ways you never imagined. You will discover courage and strength that you only previously admired in others: your voice is clearer, your resolve is stronger and your commitment unshakable. You will look in the mirror, sometimes looking a bit worn out but definitely no worse for the wear because you have learned lessons only other people on this wild journey have learned. You will also look in the mirror and see newly found confidence, a deep respect for yourself and one courageous woman. You will discover you are traveling the hero's journey, your path a shining beacon for others who are willing to travel this path with you – and lo and behold, you realize you're living your dream and you're a role model for others with similar dreams.

Inspiration Library

Music
Raise Your Glass by Pink
Applause by Lade Gaga
You Gotta Be by Des'ree
Stronger by Kelly Clarkson
Video by India.Arie

Movies
Norma Rae
Erin Brockovich
The Help

Books
The Secret Thoughts of Successful Women by Valerie Young Ed.D
Brag! The Art of Tooting Your Own Horn Without Blowing It by Peggy Klaus
Transformational Speaking by Gail Larsen
Lean In: Women, Work, and the Will to Lead by Sheryl Sandberg
Seven Spiritual Laws of Success by Deepak Chopra

"If a woman can decide who gets the last toffee, a four year old or a six year old, she can negotiate any contract in the world." – Anita Roddick

Start a Women Entrepreneur Revolution

"Rising tide lifts all boats."

—John F. Kennedy

The revolution is here. There is no doubt that women are leaping into entrepreneurism and business ownership like never before. This is an exciting time full of new opportunities, self-growth, abundance and freedom. Technology has opened the doors for new opportunities that were not previously available and our world has become smaller and more connected. However, we need not journey alone. We need to discover ways to accelerate ever closer to our own definitions of success. We need to search out women who are living the lives, running the companies, and being all-around amazing examples of what we desire for ourselves. We need to know and share that there isn't just one way to be successful, but more like ten thousand different ways to find success and to live your purpose. We need to share our struggles, challenges, successes and strategies with one another and to help one another in deep and meaningful ways. You are not alone. I'm not alone. We are already deeply connected by our common journey, so let's find ways to set out together.

As you venture forth on your journey, remember that you are already a role model in the making. You are influencing the women around you and perhaps inspiring others to take the leap. Remember how far you've already come from just that inkling of an idea or a question posed out of curiosity. You have taken thousands of steps and have learned much along the way. Give back and help others out who are a few steps behind you. Be a beacon, showing them what's possible with a bit of hard work and a ton of tenacity.

Let's not quietly work in isolation. Connect with others often. Let's seek out mentors and turn around and be mentors to others. We're all in this together, so let's start acting like it.

You give others the belief that what they seek is possible. Belief is powerful fuel. It can make the impossible, possible. It can make someone without a shot in hell, create the life only a few people can ever imagine. Belief is potent beyond words and actions. As someone who is out there doing it and architecting the life you desire, you give others a powerful gift. You give them a glimmer of possibility. You give them hope that their closeted dreams can indeed become real. You are a sparkling example of "what if." This new and grand responsibility cannot be treated lightly. Embrace your new position in the world, proudly stand up, share your gifts, extend a hand to your sisters and proclaim: "You can do it, too!"

W.E. Revolution Manifesto

Seek out role models, they have lessons to share
Stand up, be seen
Speak up
Show up
Support your peers, friends *and* competitors
Embrace this wild, unknowing path
Discover your personal definition of balance
Do the inner work, your outer work will thank you
Get out of your own way
Value yourself
Know you belong here
Define what success means to you
Magic happens outside your comfort zone
Find your tribe – they're waiting for you
Realize your business is one of the greatest personal development exercises
Acknowledge your fears and stroll on past them
Failures are lessons and potential opportunities

Constantly look for ways to grow and learn

Think big, and then think about ten times bigger than that

Learn from your mistakes and move on

Don't go it alone

Ask for help

Receive graciously

Be grateful, be grateful, be grateful

Learn from others

Share with others openly and honestly

Have faith in the process

Build together

Hire others

Delegate what you don't like doing

Have fun

Real success takes time. Don't expect it overnight

Courage is contagious so spread it

Discover your unique voice and use it for good

Know you're probably already a role model for others

Be a mentor

The greater your commitment, the greater your motivation

Celebrate frequently

Be a cheerleader for others

Listen to others, but heed to your inner wisdom

Know that tomorrow is always a new day

Flirt with risk and love uncertainty

Become a champion for other women

No boulder is too large when others help you push it

It's okay to not know the answers — go find them

Take steps daily

Give back often

If you don't love it, dump it

Perfectionism derails success

Help others by helping them believe in themselves

Everything is a choice

Passion is the antidote for fear
Enthusiasm draws people in, generosity makes them stay
Find your flow
Unearth your priorities to find your true balance
Discipline can spark creativity
Always listen to your gut – it's wiser than you give it credit
Follow the deep knowingness – it was not mistakenly given
    to you
Go after it whole-heartedly
Be the very best You
Believe in yourself
Be a role model for others

CHAPTER 9

Gems of Wisdom

Alexandra Franzen
Alexandra Franzen, Inc

"When it comes to my business – the projects I choose to pursue, the blog posts I choose to write, even the clients I choose to serve – I focus on what feels easy, simple and exciting. If it triggers a wave of resentment, it's a NO. My advice? Focus on what feels easy. Ease is a sign that you're on the right path."

Female Role Models: Ellen DeGeneres

Alison Bailey Vercruysse
18 Rabbits

"Over-thinking is a killer to entrepreneurs. Just do it!"

Female Role Models: Joy Chen

Allison Ouellet
CelerAscent

"No matter the industry you're in, you need to make your business your own. That doesn't necessarily mean you need to reinvent the wheel. Ask yourself whether it is something you can create from scratch or look at other industries to see what they've done and borrow from other successful entrepreneurs."

Female Role Models: Lt. Governor Sue Ellspermann, Marie Forleo

Amanda Johnson
True To Intention

"Follow your heart, not formulas given to you. Formulas, which are common in our industry, don't allow for customization and your Soul's truest expression. In fact, they often make you question your gut and inspiration. I've had moments when I've totally ignored my business coaches who said that my plan was nuts, but it was in those moments that I doubled and tripled my income and increased brand loyalty like nobody's business. I believe that's because my Soul really does know best."

Female Role Models: Lisa Nichols, Ursula Mentjes

Amy Lin
Blendspace

"Take small risks to get to where you want. Take advantage of Startup Weekend and other events where you can see the community and realize your ideas are not that far-fetched."

Female Role Models: My mom, Sheryl Sandberg

Amy Riley
Shoop Consulting

"My favorite part of being an entrepreneur is the possibility of it all. It excites and scares me. It's been a very long time since

I woke up and looked at my schedule and commitment for the day and wasn't excited."

Female Role Models: My mom

Andre Feigler
Enriched Schools

"First, be truthful with yourself about your passion and honest about why you're doing what you're doing. If you're going to head down this path, build something that sets you on fire and that you have some unexplainable desire to pursue. Second, if after reflection you realize you have no choice but to honor your idea or charge at your vision – give it all you've got. Be fearless, relentless and bold in the face of inevitable failures and have the conviction that it will work. Finally and along the way, find mentors and surround yourself with people that are good, and great – those that can help you learn to fail faster and forward, stay grounded and live with compassion, and become wiser and more focused with your drive – and learn from and listen to them."

Female Role Models: My grandmother, my parents, Kira Orange Jones

Angie Chang
Women 2.0, Bay Area Girl Geek Dinners, HackBright Academy

"We need women to be more high profile. Unfortunately many women don't want to be in the lime light or are not going to ask for it. They're not willing to be more visible."

Anne McCabe-Triana
CAM Private Wealth Services

"Passion is not enough, passion is a given as it will get you through the tough times. You must have a good idea and a market for it. It comes from trial and error."

Female Role Models: My grandmother (fourth woman in U.S. to receive an MD and the first MD in Alexandria County)

Anya Fernald
Belcampo Inc.

"Don't be afraid to fail. Go balls to the wall! Don't micromanage people and if you need to fire someone, do it immediately. You're the most important person in the company."

Ariane Fisher
StoryMix Media

"My piece of advice would be to have a lot of savings for a couple of years. Live like a pauper so you are able to take more risks. You are not as effective of a leader if you're worried about money. Live lean so you can give your business more of a chance."

Female Role Models: Marina von Neumann Whitman, Mary Kay Ash

Carly Blalock
Carly and Co

"You need to be organized at some level and bring whatever idea you have to the table for it's opportunity to evolve. Your vision is as original as it came to you. Design has been around forever and most of it, if not all aspects have been done before, but you can be inspired to bring something needed or something the client doesn't even know they need yet to the project. Very important to never take out the human factor. Humans are the end-user at the end of the day. You definitely cannot rely on statistics, remember it's ultimately a human experience and you have to reach out and affect that experience."

Female Role Models: Kelly Wearstler

Cat Lincoln
Clever Girls Collective

"Get the most expensive lawyer you can afford. Good contracts make good partnerships and good clients. If you go into business make it about business."

Female Role Models: I find inspiration in people everyday, inspired by my partners and the people around me, the mentors I've worked with and the great network of female peers from when I worked at Wells Fargo.

Chantal Pierrat
Emerging Women Live

"Watch out for feeling paralyzed. When you feel stuck, just take a step. Keep putting energy into it. Do not stop taking steps! Especially with fear – take a step."

Female Role Models: Martha Graham, Arianna Huffington, Oprah Winfrey, Jane Goodall, Lynne Twist

Charisse Conanan
Smarteys

"Hold onto your sense of self. There are so many opportunities for your identity to get wrapped up with your business and opportunities for outside voices to steer you in directions away from your gut. You started a business for a reason and you saw a need. Business is only one extension of who you are."

Female Role Models: Kathryn Finney, Jeanne Sullivan, Janet Hanson

Charmaine Hammond
Hammond Group

"My advice would be to get really comfortable with 'the ask' early on. By asking (for advice, support, resources, shared influence), you avoid costly mistakes, it prevents stress and builds confidence and openness in asking in the future."

Female Role Models: My parents, Lisa Nichols, Grade 9 English teacher

Chelsea Duggan
Mile Star, Inc

"My favorite part of being an entrepreneur is my "life list". I can do anything and no one can tell me 'no'. I have a list of things to do, creative outlets and being an entrepreneur allows me to do all of them and own it."

Female Role Models: My grandmother, my mother, my best friend

Chrisanna Northrup
Chrisanna Northrup

"The one thing that makes me the most successful is I only reach out to people that I know it will be a win-win for both of us. When I call them I know they will be just as lucky to work with me as I am to work with them. I never say what I want. I tell them what I'm going to give to them, what I'm ready to give them in return."

Christiane Lemieux
Dwell Studios

"Don't be afraid. Take risks and think big. If you overanalyze things you will scale back your vision very quickly."

Female Role Models: Martha Stewart, Sheryl Sandberg, Mindy Grossman, Leslie Blodgett, Mariam Naficy, Natalie Massenet

Christina Daves
CastMedic Designs

"My best tip is that being a work-at-home mom requires scheduling office hours. During that time, you work on your business. The dishes and laundry can wait. I find I am extremely efficient during those hours, when the kids are at school, and then it's fair game of getting done what I need to for the business and working around their sports and activities."

Female Role Models: Barbara Bradley Baekgaard, Sara Blakely

Cyndi Olin
Create Your Own Luck in Love

"Keep going. Put more effort in what you're doing and it will happen for you. Clarity will come. Business may take shape differently though."

Female Role Models: Friends in my network who have lost it all and have rebuilt their lives

Cynthia Nerangis
Lemon Lime Consulting

"The fear of success can stand in the way of progress. Just get out there and make it happen!"

Female Role Models: My aunt

Danielle Wiley
Sway Group

"Find a successful business owner (in a different field) who you respect and trust and ask for all the boring referrals (accounting and insurance). It should be someone you know would only hire smart people. You are so overwhelmed when you start a business it's better to get the referrals you need from someone you trust."

Female Role Models: My grandmother and one of the few senior women at Edelman (previous employer) who happened to also go to my alma mater

Dawnie Heartwell
Gems To Success

"Absolutely know your why. Be so committed to your why. Why will this matter? Why is this important to the world? Why will this be my legacy? Waking up everyday it can be simple knowing your why. Also, if it's not fun ask yourself why you're doing it. If it's not fun, figure out how to make it fun. If disappointment, struggle and challenges envelop you, look sideways and ask yourself what one thing can I do to make this better. Ask better questions and you'll get better answers."

Female Role Models: My mother, grandmother, daughter (born deaf) and my youngest sister who taught me "Because you can!"

(she passed away at 17 years old), Michelle Cameron Coulter, Helen Vanderburg

Debra Poneman
Yes to Success

"An idea comes to you because it wants to be manifested by you. If your idea wanted to be manifested by me, it would have come to me. I believe that the Creator whispered the idea in your ear because He/She wants it manifested on earth at this time. If you don't act on it, it will go to someone else who will. So don't wait until you think you're ready. Don't wait until everything is perfectly in place. We live in a relative universe; there will always be loose ends. Loose ends and all, take action. You can course correct as you go but you can't steer a parked car...and you're never going to get anywhere if you don't pull out of the driveway."

Female Role Models: Golda Meir

Diana Rothschild
NextKids

"Believe in yourself. Create a support network and when the voices rear their ugly head seek out the advice from your mentors, peers and group of advisors. Have four people you can call any time that know you - your supporters."

Female Role Models: Sheryl Sandberg, Anne-Marie Slaughter

Dina Proctor
Madly Chasing Peace

"Never let opinions of others override your intuition. If it's the right thing in your gut, stay with it."

Female Role Models: Mother Teresa

Elaine Biech
EBB Associates Inc.

"I have been fortunate to work in a profession that's rewarding. It's easy to be successful when you are doing what you love. No one should 'have to go to work'. We should all find the perfect job so that we 'get up and go to play every day."

Female Role Models: My grandmother

Elinor Stutz
Smooth Sale

"As you grow your business, reach out to help someone else building a company. The reward is in helping another. The bonuses are attracting more people to your business and increasing your status as a leader in your field. As more people adopt this policy, we will all experience social change for the better."

Female Role Models: Debra Scott, Elizabeth Hamilton-Guarino

Elizabeth Dehn
Beauty Bets

"Entrepreneurs are hard on themselves by nature, and that contributes to their success. But if you can try to cut yourself a break once in awhile, to celebrate the wins along the way, it will make the journey more positive and a little less stressful. Don't hesitate to ask for help. Everyone needs help and no one got to where they are without it, even if they seem like a genius now. Likewise, never hesitate to help others. As women, we need to pay it forward and lift each other up at every opportunity."

Female Role Models: Sarah Von Bargen, Erin Newkirk, Sister-in-law

Erika Bloom
Erika Bloom Pilates

"Find something you really really love and do it with integrity and everything will follow."

Female Role Models: Marika Molnar, Irene Dowd

Erin Newkirk
Red Stamp

"Failure may be 'not now' or 'not that way' but not a 'no way'! Failure can lead to amazing opportunities."

Female Role Models: Joanne Wilson, Whitney Johnson, Rachel Sklar, Tara Hunt, Caterina Fake

Farhana Dhalla
Farhana Dhalla

"The idea that being an entrepreneur means that I have 'more' time with my kids is a myth... I do however have more flexibility on how I structure my life so that we can spend our time on the things that are important to us. And summers off have become important."

Female Role Models: My mom, the "unknowns" - friends and people I do business with. My circle of friends; I'm inspired by the sisters around me.

Gail Gibson Cmiel
retired (founder of Employee Assistance Services Corp)

"Be clear with financial needs, lines of credit, and loans. Also, put the right team together. Know your skills and find those who can complement you. Then, nurture them because people come first."

Female Role Models: My mom

Gemma Stone
Gemma Stone

"The quicker you find your true self the better. And, as soon as you can get help – get it!"

Female Role Models: Danielle LaPorte, Alexandra Franzen, Patti Digh, SARK, Hiro Boga and my girlfriends who walk the path together.

Halelly Azulay
TalentGrow LLC

"As for advice for those just starting out: Be courageous, believe in yourself (even if you have to 'fake it till you make it' with that self-confidence), and don't sell yourself short: you've got something that's valuable and there are people out there willing to pay for your talent. Be bold. Be authentic. Be a force to be reckoned with!"

Female Role Models: Oprah Winfrey, Marie Forleo

Heather Flett
510Families.com & Rookie Moms

"In order to have a successful partnership define your partnership in writing – clarify who does what with specific roles and responsibilities. Don't be afraid to revisit it and change it over time. Have expectations set out to head off conflict before it arises."

Female Role Models: People who are successful in my network and those I hear speak at blogging conferences

Heather Jackson
Heather Jackson Yoga

"Don't let those fear-based thoughts hold you back from your dreams and vision. It's where you get stuck. When you start get clear on why. Only you can offer it because you have unique gifts. Also when you let things drop out of balance it will show up in different ways so take time for yourself."

Female Role Models: My parents, Jackie Dumaine, Amanda Lindhout

Jackie Dumaine
The Yoga Code

"Take time for stillness. In those moments of stillness we get our best ideas. Try not to force things to happen right away, allow them to germinate and foster them."

Female Role Models: Oprah Winfrey, Marie Forleo, Danielle LaPorte, Arianna Huffington, Lisa Ling, my mom, Sarah Jenks, Elizabeth Gilbert, Seane Corn

Jadah Sellner
Simple Green Smoothies

"Build trust, be consistent and take imperfect action. When you focus on doing heart-centered work in the world and provide value at the same time, everyone wins. If you have an idea, launch it as soon as possible. Until you put it out there, all of it out there, you won't learn or be able to move forward."

Female Role Models: Marie Forleo, Danielle LaPorte, Nisha Moodley

Jenee Dana
FOCUS OPUS

"I wrote my bestselling and award-winning book "Have Fun & Get It Done" so students and entrepreneurs can STOP managing their time. Time management is not effective. Define your values and priorities and design your business and LIFE around what matters most to you. Don't forget to schedule your "do nothing" and "fun" activities first. And remember, you are not perfect you are awesome."

Female Role Models: Maya Angelou, Sheri Fink, Amanda Johnson, Cathy Lee, Christine Camp, Joni B. Redick-Yundt, Alexandra Franzen, Ursula Mentjes

Jennifer Ferguson
Symphony Financial Team

"I surround myself with positive and encouraging people. I also understand that you have to do the things that need to do be done whether you feel like it or not. To paraphrase a famous Olympian, (Peter Vidmar), You have to do two things to be an Olympian, work out when you feel like it and work out when you don't.""

Jennifer Zeszut
Beckon Inc.

"Don't do it until you're certain that you feel inside that 'this is it!'. You must be certain because you'll have a tough time convincing others like investors and customers. You need to feel it in your bones."

Jenny Blake
Jenny Blake Enterprises

"Build and your courage will follow. Sometimes we tell ourselves 'when I have courage then I can quit'. We wait for courage as though it's going to rain down on us all of a sudden, THEN we can move forward. My motto is 'Live big – start small.' Take one small brave step each day."

Female Role Models: Martha Beck, Pamela Slim, Suze Orman (in college)

Jeryl Brunner
freelance writer

"Keep a very open mind. Be open to any possibility. Be intrepid and don't take it personally if someone turns you down, try another avenue. Get rid of tunnel vision and look at other possibilities that arise."

Female Role Models: Ruth Reichl, I admire artists, writers and great storytellers

Jess Butcher
Blippar

"Stop benchmarking yourself against other successful entrepreneurs or business people – it wastes valuable energy! Your personality and circumstances are unique and there is no right or wrong way to grow an innovative business. Yes, learn from others' experiences and be inspired by them, but also make your own rules and navigate your own path."

Female Role Models: Margaret Thatcher

Jill Dailey McIntosh
The Dailey Method

"The advice I'd give to people starting out is to make sure you know yourself and what your strengths are in order to best define what you can do successfully. Also to find something that you love to do or are passionate about creating. It will not only guide you towards greater success but also personal fulfillment within that success."

Female Role Models: My first dance teachers and the other women who own Dailey Method studios.

Jill Douka
Uniqueness Development Group

"My advice is to believe in yourself as much as possible and never to give up. There is always a way. You may need to change the approach, get feedback or try again, but never give up on your dreams. When you focus on what you love doing, and don't give up miracles happen. Then you need to be ready for the launch!"

Female Role Models: Arianna Huffington, Oprah Winfrey

Jill Salzman
The Founding Moms

"Don't over think launching your biz. People are very good at talking themselves right out of it. Just dive in, get it done and start."

Female Role Models: Sara Blakely, Barbra Streisand

Joanne Wilson
Gotham Gal and angel investor

"Celebrate each other! We all have self doubt."

Julie Azuma
Different Roads to Learning

"My favorite part of being an entrepreneur is the creativity of visualizing other ways to support the kids, the collaboration with amazing people and the enthusiasm and excitement of putting it together."

Female Role Models: Bonnie Wong, Yuri Kochiyama

Karen Katz
Property Management One & Mind in Motion

"Go for it. Life is short. Live with no regrets. Fit everything in and make it happen. Find your passion - dream it and live it."

Kassie Rempel
Kassie's Closet & Lillybee

"Know your way around an Excel spreadsheet. You need to know the basics of a P&L and a balance sheet. You need to get sophisticated with the un-sexy stuff."

Female Role Models: Elouise Pepion Cobell

Kathy Korman Frey
The Hot Mommas Project

"You need to love it, or something about it. It needs to drive you. Every other piece of advice follows that. You'll be willing to do all the rest of it if you love it (most days)."

Female Role Models: Rosabeth Moss Kanter and my five cool moms list. This is a list I developed when I was pregnant. I try to keep, at all times, a list of five cool moms...which is now "five cool friends." This is more than role models. This is a break-in-case-of emergency+girlfriend+mentor+role model list.

Kellee Khalil
Lover.ly

"Learn as much as you can. Use every opportunity to learn. Be open to feedback, don't take it personally. Be open to learning, growing and evolving."

Female Role Models: Joanne Wilson. Female entrepreneurs a few steps ahead of me: Hayley Barna and Katia Beauchamp of BirchBox and Alexis Maybank and Alexandra Wilkis Wilson of Gilt Groupe.

Kim Robinson
author, For Underdogs Only

"You have to listen to others but use your own authenticity as your guide. If it's good for someone else doesn't mean it is right for you. If it's not working for you, find another way."

Female Role Models: My friend, Gail.

Kimberly Wilson
Tranquil Space

"Start small, grow organically and take time to replenish the well and to refresh. Think big but start small, dip toe in first to discover if you even like it. Establish boundaries which can be tough particularly for women."

Female Role Models: Martha Stewart, Madonna, Eileen Fisher

Laura Martella
Gentleman Norman

"Just keep going even if you're afraid. Don't listen to the negative in your head If it's in your heart, follow it!"

Female Role Models: Oprah Winfrey, Bethenny Frankel

Laura Slezinger
Venture Gained Legal

"Push through when things seem difficult and discouraging. It's easy to say and difficult to do. Anchoring yourself in your values is crucial. Know who you are, what you believe and stick with it even when you will hear all sorts of voices that seem reasonable when things aren't going the way you'd like."

Female Role Models: Nnena Ukuku, Catherine Slezinger

Lily Szajnberg
GAGE

"Don't lose sight of your original idea. It is easy to get bogged down and distracted. Keep in mind the end game."

Female Role Models: My mom, my aunt, Goldie "Red" Burns, Nancy Hechinger

Loretta Love Huff
Emerald Harvest Consulting

"Make sure it is something you love doing. You have to love it because running a business is a lot of work. You will work harder on your own company than working for others, but it feels different. You are building something for yourself and your legacy.

Invest in yourself to learn what you need from people who have similar values who have accomplished what you want to have."

Female Role Models: Lisa Sasevich, Kendall SummerHawk, C.J. Hayden

Lori Saitz
Zen Rabbit

"Lots of people give up but the goal is reachable. They don't believe in themselves. True entrepreneurs don't ever give up because real success is around the next corner."

Female Role Models: Katie Couric, Oprah Winfrey

Lynn Perkins
Urban Sitter

"Know that achieving what you want will take more money and more time than you'll ever think it will. Absorb the feedback right way because it will help. You will get a lot of feedback when you start telling people about your business. It can be helpful and distracting. Absorb the feedback, decide if it modifies your plans, and quickly move on."

Female Role Models: Julia Hartz, my parents, Laney Whitcanack

Mandela Schumacher-Hodge
Tioki

"Make sure it's something you really really love before you go and share your ideas, get feedback before the prototypes and before the team. Have an internal conversation as to why you are doing it. Ask yourself is it for fame, for money or are you really excited about it and it's aligned with who you are."

Female Role Models: My mother and the people closest to me in life that I know so well, so deeply. I have seen their character.

Marci Harris
POPVOX

"Mental chatter (worry, self-doubt) creeps in when perspective narrows, when you get concerned about yourself, your ego, your fears. The only way to counter that is to think about others: the team, the people who use your product, the larger vision, the whole 'why we are doing this in the first place' thing."

Maria Johnson
De Novo Legal

"The most important thing is to build a network and strong relationships and follow up on a regular basis. Send Christmas cards and holiday greetings. I've never lost touch with the people I've met through the years. I send out 300-400 holiday cards a year and it's priceless. There is a bigger value."

Female Role Models: Gayle King

Maria Ross
Red Slice

"Too many women entrepreneurs suffer from analysis paralysis. Just get something out there! Eighty percent of something is better than 100% of nothing – then you have something you can tweak and test so you're at least moving forward. Stuck? Ask for help. No one is an expert at everything and you don't have to go it alone."

Female Role Models: Katharine Hepburn, Katie Couric, Sheryl Sandberg, Nell Merlino, Jessica Alba, Melody Bringer, Whitney Keyes, Arianna Huffington

Marissa Levin
Information Experts

"Leave the ego at the door, embrace all offers from others and ask for help. Also be part of a community."

Female Role Models: Michelle Obama. I'm also surrounded by really great women - so intellectual and they all have family as a priority.

Mary Elizabeth Wakefield
Chi-Akra Center

"Follow your passion, do what calls loudly and listen to what it is saying. Create and do what feeds you. Find a way for your dreams to sustain you in the world, monetarily. Allow yourself to receive help from others and also give to others. You can't do it all by yourself, share the dream. Be bold, be brave and embrace your dreams."

Female Role Models: My mother and my aunt, Hildegard of Bingen, Lillian Bridges

Mauria Finley
Citrus Lane

"Hire the absolute best people you can get. Put amazing people behind your company and your dream."

Female Role Models: I have a group of women CEO friends who all have different strengths than me. I also have a supportive group - a web of people and friends - who help each other out.

Megan Burns
Operations Strategy Consulting and The Naptime CEO

"I wish I had surrounded myself with wise advisers sooner than I did. When I started my firm, I used the 'lone wolf' theory thinking that through sheer determination and fierce will I could do it all on my own."

Female Role Models: Carrie Wilkerson

Meg Gill
Golden Road

"I took risks, I didn't know I was even taking risks and I didn't realize I was blindly challenging the norm. I learned so much from my mistakes. Know that making mistakes means you're growing and that's how you'll be successful."

Female Role Models: Kim Jordan

Mia Bauer
Founder of Crumbs

"I tell people that if you have an idea and think you want to do it, you have a responsibility to do it. An idea is a gift and it's rare. Never knowing would be torture. Living life with regrets is worse than a business that failed."

Female Role Models: There are many role models in politics. Same skill set as a successful business owner.

Michelle James
The Center for Creative Emergence

"Give yourself space, time, and attention to hear your inner source of guidance. Let it surprise you. And, don't believe anyone else's fears – the naysayers – it's a reflection of their fears."

Michelle Long
Bloom Retreat

"Don't give up. Have faith in yourself. Surround yourself with women who get you. You need that. It keeps you in check."

Female Role Models: Linda Bark, Cindy Turner, Marie Forleo, women in my Mamapreneur Mastermind group

Nisha Moodley
Fierce Fabulous Free

"Get into sisterhood. If you already have it in your life then go deeper. Entrepreneurship is one of the most important tools for growth and transformation and creates incredible opportunities, but it can also create incredible emotional roller coasters. It will challenge every part of you and bring all of your insecurities to the surface. Many women go through it alone – focusing narrowly on their business – and are not really open with their friends, leaving them feeling isolated and confused. So, have really incredible sisterhood in your life. Invite them to lean on you and lean on them too."

Female Role Models: Women who are mothers and who are active, engaged and present in their lives as well as in their business, Marie Forleo, Danielle LaPorte, my mom

Patty Lennon
Mom Gets A Life

"Don't make speed the name of the game. Embrace the process and understand that greatness doesn't happen overnight. Creating something extraordinary takes time. You must have faith that everything else will follow."

Female Role Models: My mom, my two children, Ellen DeGeneres

Rachel Brown
Rachel Brown Jewelry

"If you feel passion, no matter what anyone else says, passion will drive you. Even if you end up not where you thought you'd be, you'll end up in the right place. With passion you can't go wrong so don't give up."

Female Role Models: Donna Karan

Randy Peyser
Author One Stop

"Based on advice from my mentor, Jill Lublin, go attend four different networking events every month where the people are new to you each time. Bring plenty of business cards. Show up!"

Female Role Models: Jill Lublin, Kelly O'Neil

Rebecca Keller
Gravitas Publications Inc.

"You need to be clear on what you will do and what you won't do. It's easy to be working 80 hours a week without clear boundaries which can impact your relationship and physical health. Also, check in with your fears. It can be really intimidating. If you can approach it compassionately, fear dissipates and then you can find the confidence to move forward.

Female Role Models: Margaret Thatcher

Sally McGraw
Already Pretty

"For me, having a diverse group of activities bringing in money is the best thing. Also talk to people. People are your greatest resources. You're not going to do it alone. Ask for help. Ask questions. Ask for support and you'll build bridges. These people will become your foundation."

Female Role Models: My 2nd-4th grade teacher, Lisa Meyer

Sandra Baptiste
The Business Growth Agent

"Get a mentor! Get someone to talk to (not friends) and who are not involved and no emotional ties. It'll cut your journey in half."

Female Role Models: Oprah Winfrey, Arianna Huffington, Michelle Obama, Ali Brown, Fabienne Fredrickson

Sarah Hernholm
Whatever It Takes

"Become more self-aware and know who you are. Focus on what you can give more than what you can get. Express not impress. Expect good and for miracles to occur and for things to shift in the right direction."

Female Role Models: My parents

Sarah Morgan
Silly Grrl

"Stay in your bubble and do what makes YOU happy. Stop watching everyone else so much. Keep an eye on them, use it for inspiration and motivation, but don't change your direction because of it."

Female Role Models: Oprah Winfrey, Marie Forleo, Danielle LaPorte, Sarah Von Bargen, Alexandra Franzen

Sarah Von Bargen
Sarah Von Bargen

"Do what you say you'd do. Meet deadlines. Meet budgets. Read contracts and deliver on time. It's amazing how many people don't do this. Talent is 30%, success rests in the hustle and reliable hard work."

Female Role Models: Jane Pratt, Tina Fey, Amy Poehler, Mindy Kaling, Anne Lamott, Ellen DeGeneres, Miranda July

Shaherose Charania
Women 2.0

"Plan the logistics and have enough money set aside and the plan B figured out. This will reduce stress. Also, think but don't think too much as it's paralyzing. Just get started. Think less."

Sharon Schneider
Moxie Jean

"As the CEO/founder, it's your job to manage everyone else. You need someone to proactively check in with you and your emotional well-being. They are willing to ask you and you are willing to be honest."

Shawne Duperon
Shawne TV

"Get cash flow handled. Be sure to have at least 3 primary clients so you can generate and play in marketing. Don't borrow money for PR. Cash flow is king and lowers fear so you can play."

Sheri Fink
The Whimsical World of Sheri Fink

"Don't worry what people think. They don't know what you're capable of. You have an idea for a reason and you are to birth that idea into the universe."

Female Role Models: Ellen DeGeneres, Oprah Winfrey, Katy Perry

Stella Grizont
WOOPAAH

"Listen to yourself. Develop listening skills so you're aware of your voice rather than what fear is telling you. Be clear on what your inner guidance is telling you. Things are going to change and the only constant is your listening skills to what is appropriate for you at that moment. You're going to be great!"

Female Role Models: While a leader in Ladies Who Launched, I interviewed amazing women entrepreneurs every month. Also I was inspired by the women in the incubator and the workshop students. Additionally: Lexi Funk, Gale Epstein, and Lida Orzeck

Stephanie Armstrong
I Choose Love

"Follow your heart and take that step forward. Get clear on your values and strengths, and then get out there and ask, 'How can I help?'. When you do, you will find people who are values-aligned and whose skills and experience complement yours. There are a lot of people out there who want to help and collaborate. Don't wait until you're perfect; just take the first step."

Female Role Models: Summer Sanders, Brené Brown, Marianne Williamson, Sheryl Sandberg

Sue Chen
NOVA Medical Products

"What motivates me is getting to know the people that I serve. They have lost limbs, have MS or other diseases. They're courageous beautiful people."

Female Role Models: Hilary Clinton, Indra Nooyi

Suzi Pomeranz
Innovative Leadership International LLC

"Don't give up, you can do it. Breakdowns are just opportunities in disguise. Trust yourself."

Female Role Models: Oprah Winfrey, Hilary Clinton, Marie Forleo

Tami Dempsey
Hungry Hearts 4 God

"Our greatest impact lies in who we BE--not in what we DO. Discover your BIG WHY, the difference your BEING was intended to make, the reason you're here...now, at this time in history. Dare to dream that divine dream, the dream God placed in you while you were yet in the womb—it's your purpose, your value, and the gift you were designed to BE to this world. Invest in coaching that will keep you living authentically and in alignment with this calling. 'For when we live true to His intention, all the rest is added to us.' (Matthew 6:33, Pastor Tami Translation)"

Female Role Models: Janet Steiner, Amanda Johnson, Ursula Mentjes

Tess Brustein
Smarter Cookie

"I jumped in so fast that there is still so much to learn. My advice is that when you're starting out, talk to as many people as you can, do as much research as possible, experiment, build products, keep listening. It's like a science experiment."

Female Role Models: My mom, women founders in EdTech, Amy Lin

Tina Calloway
Urban FarmGirls Garden Design Co.

"Success to me is doing fulfilling, happy work that is meaningful, that helps others & benefits the community I live in, is purposeful, creative while supporting myself and my daughter. I'm also giving back by providing jobs to others in my community which is very important to me."

Female Role Models: My parents, my grandmother, Andrea Schwartz, Oprah Winfrey, Baylor Chapman

Traci Des Jardins
Restaurateur and Chef

"My advice is to know the jobs of all your people and understand their issues and the processes. Also, love what you do because you're going to work hard."

Female Role Models: Hard to pick just one. I've had lots of mentors, direct role models, help me along the way. Women are much more instrumental in exchange of information - more forthcoming.

Ursula Mentjes

Sales Coach Now

"Be disciplined with time and focus on what you want to create. We use a lot of effort in the beginning because we need to do what it takes. You have to get it off the ground no matter what. Challenges will come up but you have to be disciplined and persevere."

Female Role Models: Eleanor Roosevelt, Bethenny Frankel, Loral Langemeier

Valerie Wicks
author, Seven Spectral

"Growing up in the '90s, it was really popular to hear 'follow your dreams and they'll come true' but becoming an adult in the recession I realized you can't just 'follow' your dreams. You have to forge them. It's not just about dreaming big but going out and doing it – the sweat, the hard work. But it is completely worth it."

Female Role Models: Sheri Fink, my mother, JK Rowling

Whitney Johnson
Rose Park Advisors and Dare to Dream

"Women are saying they want to bring up the next generation. This involves more than a one-off chat over a coffee. It's a willingness to sponsor, even risk some of our political capital on their behalf."

Whitney Kell
Whitney Kell

Having an accountability coach can help keep you on track when things get tough. They can help you review what you're doing and help you be realistic with your time line holding you accountable to what you said you want. You can always improve just take massive action and look for opportunities to get uncomfortable and grow from them! Celebrate your mistakes, improve your skills by practicing & never Never Never give up!

Female Role Models: Jean Greaves, Alison Armstrong

Whitney Moss
Rookie Moms & 510Families

"Be protective of your time. You can't lose a whole day doing something that doesn't grow your business."

Female Role Models: Andrea Scher

End Notes

Introduction

MacNeil, Natalie. "Entrepreneurship Is The New Women's Movement, " *Forbes*. 08 June 2012. Web.

Slaughter, Anne-Marie. "Why Women Still Can't Have It All," *The Atlantic*. 13 June 2012. Web.

Sandberg, Sheryl. *Lean In: Women, Work, and the Will to Lead*. Knopf, 2013.

American Express Open, "The 2013 State of Women-Owned Businesses Report. A Summary of Important Trends, 1997–2013."

United Census Bureau. 2011 U.S. Census Survey data. http://quickfacts.census.gov/qfd/states/36/3651000.html

PART ONE: Importance of Role Models to Your Success

Chapter 1: What's a Role Model, Anyway?

Kalleberg, Radnvald. "Robert K. Merton: A Modern Sociological." *Classic Journal of Classical Sociology*, July 2007 7: pp 131-136, Web.

Calhoun, Craig. *Robert K. Merton: Sociology of Science and Sociology as Science*. Columbia University Press. 2010. Web.

Gibson, Donald E. "Role models in career development: New directions for theory and research." *Journal of Vocational Behavior* 65.1 (2004): 134-156.

Bosma, Niels, et al. "Entrepreneurship and role models." *Journal of Economic Psychology* 33.2 (2012): 410-424.

Obschonka, Martin, Rainer K. Silbereisen, and Eva Schmitt-Rodermund. "Entrepreneurial intention as developmental outcome." *Journal of Vocational Behavior* 77.1 (2010): 63-72.

Singh, Val, Susan Vinnicombe, and Kim James. "Constructing a professional identity: how young female managers use role models." *Women in Management Review* 21.1 (2006): 67-81.

United States Department of Commerce. United States Census Bureau. 2010 U.S. Census Survey data. http://www.census.gov/2010census/

Klein, Karen. "Nell Merlino on What Holds Women Entrepreneurs Back" *Bloomberg Businessweek*. 02, July 2010. Web.

Brizendine, Louann. *The female brain*. Random House Digital, Inc., 2007.

Hoyt, Crystal L. Simon, Stefanie. "Female Leaders Injurious or Inspiring Role Models for Women?" *Psychology of Women Quarterly* 35 1 (2011): 143-157.

Latu, Ioana M., Schmid Mast, Marianne, Lammers, Joris, Bombari, Dario. "Successful female leaders empower women's behavior in leadership tasks." *Journal of Experimental Social Psychology* 49 (2013) 444-448.

Serafin, Tatiana. "C-Suite Sees More Female Leaders Reaching Top" *Forbes*. 08 March 2013. Web

Ferriss, Timothy. *The 4-Hour Workweek: Escape 9-5, Live Anywhere, and Join the New Rich*. Crown Publishing Group. 2007.

United States Department of Labor. Bureau of Labor Statistics. 2012.

Chapter 2 Why Do I Need a Role Model?

Tharp, Twyla. *The Creative Habit: Learn It and Use It for Life*. Simon & Schuster. 2003.

Dweck, Carol. *Mindset: The new psychology of success*. Random House Digital, Inc., 2006.

Chopra, Deepak. *Creating Abundance: The A-Z Steps to a Richer Life*. Amber-Allen Publishing. 1998.

Gladwell, Malcolm. *Outliers: The story of success*. Penguin UK, 2009.

PART TWO: Modeling Success

Chapter 3: Get Out of Your Own Way (Mindset)

Murphy, Joseph. *The Power of Your Subconscious Mind*. Prentice Hall Press. 2009.

Pressfield, Steven. *The War of Art: Break Through the Blocks and Win Your Inner Creative Battles*. Black Irish Entertainment LLC. 2012.

Caprino, Kathy. "10 Lessons I Learned from Sara Blakely That You Won't Hear in Business School" *Forbes*. 23, May 2012. Web.

White, Belinda. "Spanx billionaire Sara Blakely shares her most mortifying moment" *The Telegraph*. 04, May 2012. Web.

Taylor, Colleen. "Fail Week: When Mariam Naficy's Startup Launch Was So Bad She Almost Gave The Investor Money Back" *TechCrunch*. 07, August 2013. Web.

Seligman, Martin E. *Learned optimism: How to change your mind and your life*. Random House Digital, Inc., 2011.

Dweck, Carol. *Mindset: The new psychology of success*. Random House Digital, Inc., 2006.

Seligman, Martin EP. *Flourish: A visionary new understanding of happiness and well-being*. Simon and Schuster, 2012.

Roddick, Anita. *Business as Unusual: The Triumph of Anita Roddick*. Thorsons. 2000.

Chapter 4: Get Clear (Motivation)

Sinek, Simon. *Start with Why: How Great Leaders Inspire Everyone to Take Action*. Penguin. 2009.

Sassman, Brooke. "My Greatest Challenges. An Exclusive Interview with Jessica Herrin" Savor: Business Edition: Rock the World 2013. *Savor the Success.* 08, May 2013. 8-10.

Ben-Shahar, Tal. *Happier: Can You Learn to be Happy?.* McGraw-Hill, 2008.

Sheldon, Kennon, Lyubomirsky, Sonja. "Achieving Sustainable Gains in Happiness: Change Your Actions, not Your Circumstances" *Journal of Happiness Studies.* March 2006, Volume 7, Issue 1, 55-86.

Danner, Deborah D., David A. Snowdon, and Wallace V. Friesen. "Positive emotions in early life and longevity: findings from the nun study." *Journal of personality and social psychology* 80.5 (2001): 804.

Steptoe, Andrew, Jane Wardle, and Michael Marmot. "Positive affect and health-related neuroendocrine, cardiovascular, and inflammatory processes." *Proceedings of the National academy of Sciences of the United States of America* 102.18 (2005): 6508-6512.

Das, Sajal, and James H. O'Keefe. "Behavioral cardiology: recognizing and addressing the profound impact of psychosocial stress on cardiovascular health." *Current atherosclerosis reports* 8.2 (2006): 111-118.

Brash, Joanna, Yee, Lareina. "Unlocking the full potential of women in the US economy" McKinsey & Company. April 2011.

Hewlett, Sylvia Ann, Buck Luce, Carolyn, Servon, Lisa J., Sherbin, Laura, Shiller, Peggy, Sosnovich, Eytan, Sumberg, Karen. "The Athena factor: Reversing the brain drain in science, engineering, and technology." Harvard Business School, 2008.

Chapter 5: Get Going (Behavior)

"Twenty years from now you will be more disappointed by the things that you didn't do than by the ones you did do, so throw off the bowlines, sail away from safe harbor, catch the trade winds in your sails. Explore, dream, discover."

This quote has been attributed to Mark Twain, but the attribution cannot be verified. The quote should not be regarded as authentic. The earliest documented publication of the quote is in H. Jackson Brown Jr.'s P. S. I Love You (Rutledge Hill Press, 1990).

Kaiser Thelin, Emily. "The Locavore Empire of Anya Fernald" *Food & Wine Magazine*. January 2012.

Allen, David. *Getting things done: The art of stress-free productivity*. Penguin. com, 2002.

Campbell, Chellie. *The Wealthy Spirit: Daily Affirmations for Financial Stress Reduction*. Sourcebooks, 2002.

Stainer, Michael Bungay. *Do More Great Work: Stop the Busywork, and Start the Work That Matters*. Workman Publishing, 2010.

Csikszentmihalyi, Mihaly. *Flow: The psychology of happiness*. Random House, 2013.

King, Stephen. "On Writing: A Memoir of the Craft." 2000.

Wise, Anna. *The High-Performance Mind: Mastering Brainwaves for Insight, Healing, and Creativity*. GP Putnam's Sons, 200 Madison Avenue, New York, NY 10016, 1995.

Gladwell, Malcolm. *Outliers: The story of success*. Penguin UK, 2009.

Ericsson, K. Anders, Michael J. Prietula, and Edward T. Cokely. "The making of an expert." *Harvard business review* 85.7/8 (2007): 114.

Wilde, Stuart. *Infinite Self*. Hay House, Inc, 1996.

Tharp, Twyla. *The Creative Habit: Learn It and Use It for Life*. Simon & Schuster. 2003.

Chapter 6: Get Connected (Community)

Maybank, Alexis, and Alexandra Wilkis Wilson. *By Invitation Only: How We Built Gilt and Changed the Way Millions Shop*. Penguin. com, 2012.

Ryckman, Pamela. *Stiletto Network: Inside the Women's Power Circles that are Changing the Face of Business*. Amacom, 2013.

Chapter 7: Get Energized

Hendricks, Gay. *The Big Leap: Conquer Your Hidden Fear and Take Life to the Next Level.* HarperCollins, 2009.

"How Does Heart Disease Affect Women?" U.S. Department of Health & Human Services. National Institute of Health. 26, September 2011.

Sassman, Brooke. "My Greatest Challenges. An Exclusive Interview with Jessica Herrin" Savor: Business Edition: Rock the World 2013. *Savor the Success.* 08, May 20. 8-10.

PART THREE: Stepping Up Now That You've Arrived

Chapter 8: What To Do When You've Arrived (And Long Before)

Young, Valerie. *The Secret Thoughts of Successful Women: Why Capable People Suffer from the Impostor Syndrome and how to Thrive in Spite of it.* Random House Digital, Inc., 2011.

Matthews, Gail M. "Impostor Phenomenon: Attribution for Success and Failure." *American Psychological Association, Toronto* (1984).

Gilligan, Carol. *In a different voice: Psychological theory and women's development.* Vol. 326. Harvard University Press, 1982.

Klaus, Peggy. *Brag!: the art of tooting your own horn without blowing it.* Hachette Digital, Inc., 2008.

Larsen, Gail. *Transformational Speaking.* Random House Digital, Inc., 2009.

Roddick, Anita. *Business as Unusual: The Triumph of Anita Roddick.* Thorsons. 2000.

About the Author

Jenn Aubert is a role model in-the-making and a champion for other women to be models of their best self as well.

One day shortly after having her first child, Jenn found herself laying on her apartment floor in an acute state of fear, shielding her infant son. Postpartum anxiety had surfaced quickly and it evasively took over her life. Fearing leaving the house, she created catastrophic scenarios and used creative stories to avoid business and social commitments. Not surprisingly, her business began to struggle, and it was taking a toll on her finances and family.

How were other women managing their businesses, themselves, their families? Jenn wanted to know. She searched around but found few examples to draw on for ideas.

Realizing she had to figure this out on her own, Jenn decided to face her fears — both large and small, personal and professional. After years of wanting to be bold (but trading in her dreams to play it safe), she immediately took steps to fully reengage the world from a powerful place, leaving her fears and doubts in the dust.

Today, Jenn wants other women to be able to do the same in every area of their lives, and most especially when it comes to their roles as entrepreneurs. That's because, the way Jenn sees it, as entrepreneurs, our businesses are extensions of ourselves; and when the business is having problems, it's usually a personal problem that is at its core.

Jenn helps with just that by working with women entrepreneurs to move through their fears and self-doubts so that they can build their business and live the life of their dreams. She believes in the power of role models as a way for women to know that what they dream of is attainable, and that other women are proof of the possibility.

Because let's face it: starting a business is one of the biggest self-development challenges you'll ever undertake.

Besides living more fearlessly (always a work-in-progress), Jenn is also a licensed acupuncturist with a thriving practice in San Francisco. Always in search of her next challenge, she is launching a new company focused on connecting women entrepreneurs, providing educational tools and resources and helping women succeed in business.

Made in the USA
San Bernardino, CA
28 October 2015